The First Fifty Years

The First Fifty Years

A Jubilee in Prose and Poetry
Honoring Women Rabbis

RABBI SUE LEVI ELWELL

JESSICA GREENBAUM

RABBI HARA E. PERSON

editors

CCAR
Press

CENTRAL CONFERENCE OF AMERICAN RABBIS
NEW YORK ❧ 2023 / 5783

Library of Congress Cataloging-in-Publication Data

Names: Elwell, Ellen Sue Levi, editor. | Greenbaum, Jessica, editor. | Person, Hara, editor.

Title: The first fifty years: a jubilee in prose and poetry honoring women Rabbis / Rabbi Sue Levi Elwell, Jessica Greenbaum, and Rabbi Hara E. Person, editors.

Description: New York: Central Conference of American Rabbis, 2023. | Summary: "Contributors from across the Jewish and gender spectrums reflect on the meaning of this moment and the ensuing decades, both personally and for the Jewish community. In short pieces of new prose, authors-many of them pioneering rabbis-share stories, insights, analysis, and celebrations of women in the rabbinate. These are inter-twined with a wealth of poetry that poignantly captures the spirit of this anniversary" -- Provided by publisher.

Identifiers: LCCN 2022058492 (print) | LCCN 2022058493 (ebook) | ISBN 9780881236309 (paperback) | ISBN 9780881236316 (ebook)

Subjects: LCSH: Rabbis--United States--Office. | Women rabbis--United States--Intellectual life. | Rabbis--United States. | Women rabbis--Israel--Intellectual life. | Rabbis--Israel. | Reform Judaism--United States. | Reform Judaism--Israel. | Judaism--Functionaries.

Classification: LCC BM652 .F54 2023 (print) | LCC BM652 (ebook) | DDC 296.082--dc23/eng/20230119

LC record available at https://lccn.loc.gov/2022058492

LC ebook record available at https://lccn.loc.gov/2022058493

Published by Reform Judaism Publishing, a division of CCAR Press
Central Conference of American Rabbis
355 Lexington Avenue, New York, NY 10017
(212) 972-3636 | www.ccarpress.org

Text designed and composed by Scott-Martin Kosofsky
at The Philidor Compnay, Rhinebeck, NY

Printed in the United States of America
10 9 8 7 6 5 4 3 2 1

For Our Vatikot

This volume is a celebration of all the women,
CCAR members and former CCAR members,
who were ordained from 1972 to 1983
by Hebrew Union College–Jewish Institute of Religion
and other seminaries.

We are proud to honor all the vatikot.

Vatikot, 1972–1983

Susan Abramson
Leslie J. Alexander
Melanie Aron
Aliza Berk
Donna Berman
Miriam Biatch
Sandy K. Bogin
Lenore Bohm
Barbara Borts
Michal Bourne
Ellen Weinberg Dreyfus
Susan L. Einbinder
Jacqueline Koch Ellenson
Dena Feingold
Cathy Felix
Helene Ferris
Sally Finestone
Karen Fox
Joan Friedman
Elyse Frishman
Laura Geller
Rosalind Gold
Elyse M. Goldstein
Debra Hachen
Patrice Heller
Deborah Hirsch
Patricia Karlin-Neumann
Jan Caryl Kaufman
Bonnie Koppell
Leah Kroll
Lynne F. Landsberg, *z"l*

Devon Lerner
Ellen Lewis
Judith Lewis
Beverly W. Magidson
Janet Marder
Ilene Melamed
Michal Mendelsohn
Carole L. Meyers, *z"l*
Randi Musnitsky
Amy Perlin
Sara Rae Perman
Mindy Avra Portnoy
Sally J. Priesand
Deborah Prinz
Liz Rolle
Gila C. Ruskin
Shelia Russian
Laurie Rutenberg
Sandy Eisenberg Sasso
Kinneret Shiryon
Ruth Sohn
Myra Soifer
Karen Soria
Bonnie Steinberg
Shira Stern
Susan Berman Stone
Susan Talve
Faedra Lazar Weiss
Julie Wolkoff
Marjorie S. Yudkin, *z"l*
Deborah Zecher

~::~

Dedicated with love, respect, and pride
to our sister

Rabbi Karen Leah Fox

the daughter of Holocaust survivors
who became
the first rabbi in our family,
the first woman rabbi to serve
as a regional director at the UAHC/URJ,
the first woman rabbi at Wilshire Boulevard Temple
and at Camp Hess Kramer, Los Angeles

A rabbis' rabbi to generations of rabbis
An inspiration to our family members of all ages

RABBI STEVEN A. FOX AND VICKI REIKES FOX

Dedicated to

Rabbi Karen Fox

by her family.
We all take immense pride in her professional
and personal achievements.
She has managed to be one of the *vatikot* who not only
paved the way for the future generations of rabbis,
but also found the proper balance between
work and family.

May she progress from wisdom to courage.

MICKEY, AVI, LIZ, BENJY, JULIE,
DAVID, LENA, IZZY, AND JOE

The members and staff of

Temple Sinai, Washington, DC,

celebrate this milestone,
fifty years of ordaining women rabbis.
We honor our rabbi emerita,

Mindy Avra Portnoy (HUC-JIR, 1980),

whose tenure from 1986 to 2013 and continued
connection have shaped our community significantly.

We honor the women who have served Temple Sinai as rabbis:

Lenore Bohm (HUC-JIR, 1982)	1975 – 1977
Liz Rolle (HUC-JIR, 1981)	1978 – 1979
Sara Rae Perman (HUC-JIR, 1981)	1979 – 1981
Judith L. Brazen (HUC-JIR, 1990)	2001 – 2003
Shena Potter Jaffee (HUC-JIR, 2001)	2003 – 2007
Jessica Oleon Kirschner (HUC-JIR, 2007)	2007 – 2014
Erica Seager Asch (HUC-JIR, 2008)	2009 – 2013
Hannah L. Goldstein (HUC-JIR, 2013)	2013 – present

… those who grew up at Temple Sinai:

Karyn D. Kedar (HUC-JIR, 1985)
Shoshana Kaminsky (RRC, 1994)
Alanna Sklover (RRC, 2013)
Isaama Goldstein-Stoll (HUC-JIR, 2019)
Alexandra Stein (HUC-JIR, 2022)

… and those who enhance our community as current members:

Stephanie L. Bernstein (HUC-JIR, 2009)
Melanie Aron (HUC-JIR, 1981)

עֲשֵׂה לְךָ רַב וּקְנֵה לְךָ חָבֵר

In honor of

Rabbi Ellen Weinberg Dreyfus

We are proud of our *ima* (and *oma*) on the bimah

Your loving family,
JAMES N. DREYFUS
BEN DREYFUS AND ELIZABETH RICHMAN
YONATAN AND AVITAL RICHMAN-DREYFUS
LINA AND ADAM WALLACE, SIVAN, EITAN, AND PENINA WALLACE
DAVID DREYFUS AND LAUREN BUTTERFIELD, MAX DREYFUS

∾∷∾ ∾∷∾ ∾∷∾

In honor of

Rabbi Karen Leah Fox

the first woman rabbi in our family.

You won our hearts, our love, and especially our respect.
Your insights, kindness, and words of Torah have guided us.
We love you and are honored and thrilled to call you our sister,
Tante Karen, and especially our rabbi.

RACHEL ROSEN AND RON WEXLER
ITIYA AND PINNEY, NAF AND ANNA, JESSE,
AHUVA AND DENNIS, SHIRA AND JOSH

On behalf of our founding members,
the many congregants whose lives she has touched
and friends,

CONGREGATION B'NAI SHALOM
Westborough, Massachusetts,

shares our profound gratitude to our founding rabbi,
Rabbi Emerita Debra Hachen.

We are proud to be the first congregation in New England
to hire a woman as our rabbi, our teacher, our partner,
and guide.

~∶~ ~∶~ ~∶~

We honor
Rabbi Sally J. Priesand

and all our *vatikot*,
the first women pioneers in the rabbinate,
who pushed the limits, didn't take no for an answer,
and irrevocably changed the face of Judaism.
You became role models for all who followed,
and we are grateful to you.

THE CCAR LEADERSHIP AND STAFF

The Birken family
in honor of
Rabbi Rosalind Gold

Nancy Berman
and Alan Bloch
in honor of
Rabbi Karen Fox

Rabbis Laurie Katz Braun,
Alysa Mendelson Graf,
and Sarah Reines
in honor of Rabbi
Jacqueline Koch Ellenson

Fields Family Charitable
Fund, in honor of
Rabbi Karen Fox

Eric and Shari Fox
in honor of
Rabbi Karen Fox

Rabbi Karen Fox
in honor of
Rabbi Rosalind Gold

Steven Fraider
and Dale Perry
in honor of
Rabbi Karen Fox

Rabbi Daniel Freelander
in honor of
Rabbi Elyse Frishman

David Gold and Caryn Espo
in honor of
Rabbi Karen Fox

Rabbi Rachel Gurevitz
in honor of
Rabbi Debra Hachen and
Rabbi Dr. Deborah Hirsch

Sam Hirsch and Marti Walsh
in honor of
Rabbi Dr. Deborah Hirsch

Susan and Martin Jannol
in honor of
Rabbi Karen Fox

Rabbi Robert Leib
in honor of
Rabbi Patrice Heller and
Rabbi Lynne Landsberg, z"l

Micah Lewis-Kraus
in honor of
Rabbi Ellen Lewis

Rabbi David Lyon
in honor of our vatikot
who blazed the trail
for so many

Rabbi Amy Perlin
in honor of
Rabbi Rosalind Gold

Deborah Rivel
and David Levenfeld
in honor of
Rabbi Dr. Deborah Hirsch

Neil (z"l) and Betsey Roberts
in honor of
Rabbi Karen Fox

Roots of Reform Judaism
in honor of
Rabbi Devon Lerner

Gary and Jennifer Salomons
in honor of
Rabbi Karen Fox

Stanley Salomons
in honor of
Rabbi Karen Fox

Rabbi Dennis C. Sasso
in honor of
Rabbi Sandy Eisenberg Sasso

Elizabeth and David
Sherman
in honor of
Rabbi Dr. Deborah Hirsch

Ronny Jo Siegal
in honor of
Rabbi Ellen Lewis

Rabbi Yael Splansky
in honor of
Rabbi Dr. Deborah Hirsch

Carol Kahn Strauss
in honor of
Rabbi Karen Fox

The Temple
in honor of
Rabbi Lenore Bohm
and all of our vatikot

Temple B'nai Shalom
in honor of Founding Rabbi
Emerita Amy R. Perlin

The clergy team of
Temple Emanu-El, Dallas
in honor of all of our vatikot

Temple Solel
in honor of
Rabbi Lenore Bohm

Rabbi Michael Weinberg
in honor of
Rabbi Ellen Weinberg
Dreyfus

Stuart Williger
in honor of
Rabbi Rosalind Gold

Rabbi Joel Abraham, in honor of Rabbi Shira Stern

Leslie and Franklin Abrams, in honor of Rabbi Dr. Deborah Hirsch

Sandy and Bob Albert, in honor of Rabbi Dr. Deborah Hirsch

Janice Alper, in honor of Rabbi Karen Fox

Rabbi Ruth Alpers, in honor of all of our early women rabbis

Rabbi Renni Altman, in honor of all of our early women rabbis

Esther Ann Asch, in honor of Rabbi Dr. Deborah Hirsch

Cantor Nancy Bach, in honor of Rabbi Dr. Deborah Hirsch

Rabbi Shelley Kovar Becker, in honor of all of our early women rabbis

Rabbi Lisa Bellows, in honor of Rabbi Emerita Sally J. Priesand

Rabbi Elissa Ben-Naim, in honor of Rabbi Karen Fox

Rabbi Marc Berkson, in honor of all of our early women rabbis

Rabbi Sarah Berman, in honor of all of our early women rabbis

Rabbi Arlene Bernstein, in honor of all of our early women rabbis

Ellen Bittner, in honor of all of our early women rabbis

Gay Block, in memory of Rabbi Carole Meyers, z"l

Sandra and Bob Braun, in honor of Rabbi Karen Fox

Rabbi Carey Brown, in honor of Rabbi Dr. Joan Friedman

Rabbi Jeffrey Brown, in honor of Rabbi Lenore Bohm

The Burke family, in honor of Rabbi Karen Fox

CCAR Responsa Committee, in honor of Rabbi Dr. Joan Friedman

Chavurat Shalom of SWFL, in honor of Rabbi Myra Soifer

Rabbi Karen Companez, in honor of all of our early women rabbis

Congregation Beth El, Berkeley, CA, in honor of all of our early
women rabbis

Rabbi Julian Cook, in honor of Rabbi Emerita Sally J. Priesand

Rabbi William and Georgianne Cutter, in honor of Rabbi Karen Fox

Rabbi Stanley and Resa Davids, in honor of Rabbi Karen Fox

Rabbi Lucy Dinner, in honor of all of our early women rabbis

Rochelle and Bernie Dyme, in honor of Rabbi Dr. Deborah Hirsch

Rabbi Denise Eger, in honor of all of our early women rabbis

Fred and Eileen Eichler, in honor of Rabbi Dr. Deborah Hirsch

Ariel, Natanel, Paul, and Nava Ervin, in honor of Rabbi Myra Soifer

Michael and Ellen Feingold, in honor of Rabbi Myra Soifer

Rabbi Marla Feldman, in honor of all of our early women rabbis

Sue and Steve Feldman, in honor of Rabbi Dr. Deborah Hirsch

Tobi Mackler and Steven Fischer, in honor of Rabbi Myra Soifer

Adam Fox, in honor of Rabbi Karen Fox

Bailey Reikes Fox, in honor of Rabbi Karen Fox

Ellen and Steve Fox, in honor of Rabbi Lenore Bohm

Abraham Fox-Rosen, in honor of Rabbi Karen Fox

Benjy, Julie, David, Lena, and Josef Fox-Rosen, in honor of
Rabbi Karen Fox

Sue Fredericks, in honor of Rabbi Dr. Deborah Hirsch

Rabbi Lawrence Freedman, in honor of Rabbi Bonnie Koppell

Gary and Georgia Freedman-Harvey, in honor of Rabbi Karen Fox

Cheryl and Barry Fulmer, in honor of Rabbi Myra Soifer

Rabbi Ruth Gais, in honor of Rabbi Ellen Lewis

Rabbi David Gelfand, in honor of Rabbi Emerita Sally J. Priesand

Rabbi Matthew Gewirtz, in honor of Rabbi Ellen Lewis

Matt and Monica Glicken, in honor of Rabbi Dr. Deborah Hirsch

Rabbi Paul Golomb, in memory of Rabbi Lynne Landsberg, z"l

Rabbi Linda Henry Goodman, in honor of Class of 1985

Laurie Goodman and Don Spetner, in honor of Rabbi Karen Fox

Rabbi Jodie Gordon, in honor of Rabbi Deborah Zecher

Rabbi Deena Gottlieb, in honor of Rabbi Ellen Lewis

Rabbi Danny Gottlieb, Rabbi PJ Schwartz, and Cantor Devorah
    Felder-Levy, in honor of Rabbi Melanie Aron

Rabbi Amanda Greene, in honor of Rabbis Wendi Geffen, Lisa Greene,
    Rachel Timoner, Sara Mason-Barkin, Leah Lewis, and Sally J. Priesand

Grace Cohen Grossman, in honor of Rabbi Karen Fox

Jeff and Sharon Hershow, in honor of Rabbi Karen Fox

Rabbis Neil Hirsch and Jodie Gordon, in honor of Rabbis Elyse Frishman,
    Deborah Hirsch, Shira Stern, and Deborah Zecher

Robin Hirsch, in honor of Rabbi Dr. Deborah Hirsch

Rabbi Lisa Hochberg-Miller, in honor of all of our early women rabbis

Jacobson-Glicken-Romeyn crew, in honor of Rabbi Dr. Deborah Hirsch

Rabbi Howard Jaffe, in honor of all of our early women rabbis

Mark Jay, in honor of Rabbi Ellen Lewis

Rabbi Bruce Kadden, in honor of all of our early women rabbis

Rabbi Yoel Kahn, in honor of all of our early women rabbis

Rabbi Beth Kalisch, in honor of all of our early women rabbis

Rabbi Lewis Kamrass, in honor of Rabbi Emerita Sally J. Priesand

Rabbi Debra Kassoff, in honor of Rabbi Deborah Zecher

Rabbi Jan Katzew, in honor of all of our early women rabbis

Cantor Todd Kipnis, in honor of Rabbi Dr. Deborah Hirsch

Myra Klahr, in honor of Rabbi Myra Soifer

Marianne and Garth Klimchuk, in honor of Rabbi Dr. Deborah Hirsch

Rabbi Dr. Audrey Korotkin, in honor of Rabbi Dr. Joan Friedman

Eve Landau, in honor of Rabbi Dr. Deborah Hirsch

Rabbi Eric J. Lazar, in honor of all of our early women rabbis

Susan Lentz, in honor of Rabbi Karen Fox

Karen Levin, in honor of Rabbi Ellen Lewis

Micah and Gideon Lewis-Kraus, in honor of Rabbi Ellen Lewis

Rabbi Seth Limmer, in honor of all of our early women rabbis

Rabbi Dr. Janet Liss, in honor of Rabbis Susan Abramson, Ellen Dreyfus,
   Jackie Ellenson, Karen Fox, Rosalind Gold, Joan Friedman, Deborah
   Hirsch, Ellen Lewis, Amy Perlin, Sally J. Priesand, Shira Stern,
   and Deborah Zecher

Rabbi Richard Litvak, in honor of all of our early women rabbis

Rabbi Emily Losben-Ostrov, in honor of all of our early women rabbis

Andrea Lowenstein, in honor of Rabbi Ellen Lewis

Rabbi Tamar Malino, in honor of Rabbi Deborah Prinz

Alison Mayersohn and Rabbi Laurence Scheindlin, in honor of
   Rabbi Karen Fox

Rabbi Barbara Metzinger, in honor of all of our early women rabbis

Mitchell and Phyllis Miller, in honor of Rabbi Karen Fox

Rabbi Leana Moritt, in honor of all of our early women rabbis

Rabbi Susan Heneson Moskowitz, in honor of all of our early
   women rabbis

Rabbi Robin Nafshi, in honor of Rabbi Rosalind Gold

Rabbi Jason Nevarez, in honor of Rabbi Lenore Bohm

Lois and Neil Nyren, in honor of Rabbi Dr. Deborah Hirsch

Chet and Peggy Pardee, in honor of Rabbi Myra Soifer

Rabbi Michelle Pearlman, in honor of all of our early women rabbis

Rabbi Michelle Pearlman, in honor of Rabbis Ellen Weinberg Dreyfus
   and Ellen Lewis

Rabbi Hara E. Person, in honor of all of our *vatikot*

Rabbi Emerita Sally J. Priesand, in honor of all my female colleagues

Rabbi Laura Rappaport, in honor of Rabbi Emerita Amy Perlin

Rabbi Fred Reiner, in honor of Rabbi Emerita Sally J. Priesand

Rabbi Daniel Reiser, in honor of Rabbi Ellen Lewis

Ethan and Sabra Rivel, in honor of Rabbi Dr. Deborah Hirsch

Buddy Rosenthal, in honor of Rabbi Ellen Lewis

Lydia Rosner, in honor of Rabbi Dr. Deborah Hirsch

Rabbi Dennis Ross, in honor of Rabbi Deborah Zecher

Barry A. Roth and Ying Przybyszewski, in honor of Rabbi Myra Soifer

Robin Rubin, in honor of Rabbi Lenore Bohm

Rabbi Arnold James and Marcia Rudin, in honor of Rabbi Myra Soifer

Carole and Sadie Sadler, in honor of Rabbi Dr. Deborah Hirsch

Julie Salamon and William Abrams, in honor of Rabbi Dr. Deborah Hirsch

Rabbi Amy Scheinerman, in honor of Rabbi Joan Friedman

Rabbi Jeremy Schneider, in honor of Rabbi Sally Finestone

Barbara Schneidman, in honor of Rabbi Dr. Deborah Hirsch

Rabbi David Segal and Cantor Rollin Simmons, in honor of
    Rabbi Elaine Glickman

Rabbi M. Beaumont Shapiro, in honor of Rabbi Karen Fox

Rabbi Richard Shapiro, in honor of the women in the ordination
    class of 1981

Rabbi Randy Sheinberg, in honor of all our early women rabbis

Shir Tivkah, in honor of Rabbi Ellen Weinberg Dreyfus

Rabbi Alexandria Shuval-Weiner, in honor of all of our early
    women rabbis

Rabbi James Simon, in honor of Rabbis Laura Geller, Janet Marder,
    and Gila Ruskin

Irene and Leon Skolnick, in honor of Rabbi Myra Soifer

Rabbi Sharon Sobel, in honor of all of our early women rabbis

Rabbi Emeritus Karen Soria, in honor of Rabbi Myra Soifer

Helene Spring, in honor of Rabbi Dr. Deborah Hirsch

Michael and Marsha Starr, in honor of Rabbi Dr. Deborah Hirsch

Rabbi Peter Stein, in honor of Rabbi Emerita Sally J. Priesand

Rabbi Eleanor Steinman, in honor of all of our early women rabbis

Rabbis Liza Stern, Debra Robbins, Rachel Goldenberg, Kimberly Herzog Cohen, Annie Bornstein, and Cantors Vicky Glikin, and Leslie Niren, in honor of Rabbi Ellen Lewis

Rabbi Micah Streiffer, in honor of Rabbi Dr. Joan Friedman

Rabbi Karen Strok, in honor of all of our early women rabbis

Temple Bat Yahm, in honor of all of our early women rabbis

Temple B'nai Israel and Rabbi Vered Harris, in honor of all of our early women rabbis

Rabbi Allison Vann, in memory of Rabbi Marjorie Yudkin, z"l

Barri and Dan Waltcher, in honor of Rabbi Dr. Deborah Hirsch

Rabbi Susan Warshaw, in honor of Rabbi Emerita Amy Perlin

Rabbi Joshua Weinberg, in honor of Rabbi Ellen Weinberg Dreyfus

Rabbi Dr. Dvora Weisberg, in honor of Rabbi Dr. Joan Friedman

Rabbi Sarah Weissman, in honor of Rabbi Janet Marder

Rabbi Michael White, in honor of all of our early women rabbis

Carole Zawatsky, in honor of Rabbi Karen Fox

Rabbi Michael Zedek, in honor of all of our early women rabbis

Suzanne Kathleen Zoss, in honor of Rabbi Myra Soifer

Contents

Poetry in italics

Introduction

RABBI HARA E. PERSON

THIS ANTHOLOGY pays tribute to the profoundly radical accomplishments of the first fifty years of women in the rabbinate. On its pages you will encounter the many currents of new thought that pool into our contemporary, collective sense of "Rabbi." On a micro scale this anthology itself also reflects the coming together of many forces, but we can locate a first one: the poet Merle Feld, commissioned by the Women's Rabbinic Network celebration to mark the fiftieth anniversary of women in the rabbinate, "The Journey to 50," with an original poem, suggested that we commission and publish a whole book of poetry celebrating women rabbis! I am grateful to Merle for her suggestion, the spark that ignited this book.

Of course, the genesis of this book goes back much farther. In many ways, it began with the groundbreaking ordination of Rabbi Sally J. Priesand in 1972 from Hebrew Union College–Jewish Institute of Religion (HUC-JIR) in Cincinnati. But we could also argue that it began with the ordination of Rabbiner Regina Jonas in Berlin in 1935. And further back again, this evolving story began with the many women who aspired to become rabbis throughout Jewish history, whose dreams were deferred by centuries of patriarchy, and who had to find alternative paths of service and leadership.

For me, this book begins on a brownstone stoop in Brooklyn, when my rabbi told me the first woman was being ordained. Until that moment, I had never thought about the fact that women couldn't be rabbis—it had just never occurred to me that that option wouldn't be open to me if that was something I wanted to do. And in that moment I was determined to meet this pioneer, this first woman rabbi, who became my hero right then and there. While it was years before I finally met Rabbi Priesand, as a child on that Brooklyn stoop

I could not have imagined what her courageous act of opening the door to the rabbinate would mean for me, both personally and professionally. That is an essential debt that can only be paid forward. I hope the publication of this book stands as part of that gratitude, and I am grateful to have Rabbi Priesand's essay, fittingly, at its start.

This collection serves as a mile marker along the journey, a momentary stopping place for reflection and commemoration. While we experience the evolution of women in the rabbinate as inevitable, that doesn't mean it was easy. These pages likewise acknowledge challenges and complexities of these fifty years, identifying some of the detours and roadblocks that still lie ahead. Alongside tremendous gains and systemic changes, pain and inequity are not yet eradicated. Women rabbis still face bias, microaggressions, pay inequity, and other obstacles. Naming challenges is one of the ways that we are able to break through the barriers that keep us from getting to the goal of equity.

The work continues. In a mere half century, rabbinic leadership effected a dramatic turning point in Jewish history, an acknowledgment that the voices that were silent or silenced, marginalized, unheard and unseen, are an essential part of the rich and variegated fabric of the Jewish story and must be included. We now claim a richness of experience that nourishes us all, individuals of all genders, identities, and roles in our Jewish communities. Becoming the most beautifully diverse, inclusive, and thriving community of our highest aspirations, we all need to know what has led us here on the path to a healthy, equitable, and flourishing future.

Today we recognize that the rabbinate is made up not only of women and men, but also rabbis with diverse gender identities. This knowledge, too, is grounded in Torah. For centuries, our scholars recognized that Genesis celebrates inclusivity: both heaven and earth and the heavenly bodies and angelic beings. God created humans and animals and everything in between. God created human beings in God's image, a full spectrum of gender expressions and sexualities. Binary thinking has blinded us to a fuller appreciation of the beauty and power of God's creations. The ongoing work of equity includes all rabbis of every identity, including the full spectrum of gender, sexual, and racial identities. One of the key learnings from these fifty years of change is that the door to opportunity and inclusion must not be opened just once with great fanfare, but must be held open continually for all who wish to enter. As Rabbi Priesand writes in her piece in this collection, "I would like to think that my opening the door for women in the Jewish community was a first step toward opening the door for all who would serve the Jewish people."

Together with my cherished coeditors Rabbi Sue Levi Elwell and Jessica Greenbaum, we are grateful to everyone who submitted a piece of prose or a poem. It was a privilege to read so many powerful words, reflections of individuals across geographical and generational divides. We are inspired by the many writers who chose to share their words with us and with you, the readers.

We want to thank everyone at CCAR Press who helped bring this collection to publication. Rafael Chaiken, director of CCAR Press, supported this project from the start. Chiara Ricisak, CCAR assistant editor, has been the person who has held this project together. Thanks also to Debbie Smilow, Raquel Fairweather-Gallie, and Rabbi Annie Villarreal-Belford. We are lucky to have such a talented team at CCAR Press. Debra Hirsch Corman and Michelle Kwitkin expertly handled copyediting and proofreading. Thank you to Brenda Baker and Barbara Leff for the cover and to Scott-Martin Kosofsky for the design.

Thanks also to Pamela Goldstein, CCAR director of advancement, and Samantha Rutter, development manager, for managing the fundraising that made this volume possible. Thanks are also due to Rabbi Steve Fox, CCAR chief executive emeritus, whose excitement about this idea provided the momentum we needed to move forward.

I want to especially thank all the many donors whose love for our *vatikot* enabled this project to come to fruition. Everyone's generosity allowed us to stop and create a place in time to hear all the voices in these pages—as we move on to the next fifty years.

Pioneers

~::~

As One Awakens after a Long Sleep

Alicia Jo Rabins

The oldest piece of literature
By an author whose name
We know is a hymn to the
Divine written by Enheduanna,
A Sumerian priestess. Which is
To say, those we call "the Ancients"
Knew some truths we moderns re-
Discovered only recently. Such as:
Women, too, are born to lead,
Hold sacred space, convene, bless,
Equally. Our ancestors forgot this
Truth for centuries, then recently
Remembered, as one awakens
After a long sleep. Fifty
Years awake, one jubilee. Fifty years,
Praise be to the One who planted
Eternal life in each of us: in her, them,
Him, in you, in me. She neither sleeps
Nor slumbers, the *Shechinah*, rather whispers
In our ears: *You may forget Me, or forget*
To recognize Me in some of You. But
This is temporary. Beneath this forgetting
Is the eternal truth: Hineinu. Hineini.

A First Step

RABBI SALLY J. PRIESAND

UPON THE FIFTIETH anniversary of my ordination, I am grateful to God that part of my life's work has been to open new doors for women in the Jewish community, but I have tried never to lose sight of the larger mission of the Jewish people, which is to derive from the words of Torah a set of values and a sense of holiness that enables us always to be partners with God in completing the world. What that means from my vantage point is not only putting the task of tikkun olam (repairing the world) in the forefront of our work, but creating a society based on equality and inclusivity. All people are created b'tzelem Elohim, in God's image. We are one human family, all of us God's children, and all of us worthy of dignity and respect and the opportunity to become all that we want to become.

When I was studying for the rabbinate, most people were conscious of only two genders, male and female; today we know there are many more—transgender, nonbinary, genderqueer—and we know too that the Jewish community is very diverse, coming as we do from many different backgrounds. Only now, for example, have we begun to welcome into our synagogues and institutions people of color and be grateful for all that they have to offer the Jewish people and humanity as a whole. Let us never forget that one of the blessings of being human is the right to identify as we wish, to know ourselves and be ourselves.

I would like to think that my opening the door for women in the Jewish community was a first step toward opening the door for all who would serve the Jewish people, and I urge the Reform Movement to act as one family and be more proactive than it has been in the past, educating ourselves and the people we serve and sharing with them the incredible possibilities that await unfolding when we welcome everyone into the fold. Doing so will benefit us all, and the Jewish community will be stronger for it.

Blessed Be the Firsts

RABBI MARY L. ZAMORE

Blessed be the women who taught and led, often without formal
recognition.

Blessed be Rabbi Regina Jonas, privately ordained in 1935 in Nazi
Germany, proving that a woman could be a rabbi. Murdered at
Auschwitz in 1944.

Blessed be the women who hoped to be rabbis, but it was not yet
to be.

Blessed be Rabbi Sally J. Priesand, publicly ordained on June 3, 1972,
by HUC-JIR. With great bravery, she created a lasting path for
women to become rabbis, eventually in all branches of Judaism.

Blessed be the women, especially our *vatikot*, who followed Rabbi
Priesand, rabbis who forged the way for the last five decades. And
blessed be our future rabbis.

Blessed be each rabbi who has been a first in her rabbinate, persever-
ing to find fulfillment and accomplishment. And we are all firsts
in myriad ways, as opportunities are not yet equal.

Blessed be the rabbis who are helping shape new understandings of
ritual, history, teaching, text, and leadership for us all.

Blessed be the classmates, teachers, mentors, partners, families, and
friends who support us.

Blessed be those who call us rabbi. Our communities and institutions
are enriched by our talents.

Blessed be you of beautiful identities who are creating new paths as
rabbis, cantors, Jewish professionals, and community members.
May you find acceptance and celebration of your leadership.

Let my people go
that we may serve You

MERLE FELD

For Sally Priesand (HUC-JIR 1972) and Lisa Feld (HCRS 2023)

Remember girdles? Remember the anger
we weren't supposed to show, or even feel?
Remember sitting and waiting to say Bar'chu
as someone counted, *Not one, not two* …
The being invisible, the tears blinked back,
fiercely. Remember the love, the innocence
assaulted, hearing for the first time, those words,

and those words, and those, such words
in a holy book, demeaning me, you, us?
All these years later, I feel the pain, rising,
constricting, afflicting. Remembering. Searching
for a reason to stay: love is stronger than death.

Tears became anger — that word — the ultimate
weapon. *She's an angry woman* (so we can
ignore her, put her down, close our ears and hearts).
Blessed be the allies, calling for the first time
from the bimah — *Taamod!* The ones who broke
through the tight circles on *Simchas Torah*

and passed us a scroll to hold, to dance with.
The ones who said *yes, yes, yes. And yes.*
And we, the wrestlers — *I won't let you go
till you bless me.* The lust, the longing, to learn,
to *leyn,* to lead, to *bensch,* to be counted, to be
called, to locate our wisdom, to inhabit our power

and our tenderness, to build holy communities,
fully and richly as ourselves, as Jewish women,
as rabbis — *I won't let you go till you bless me.*
Now, and going forward, now, and for tomorrow,
my heart soars, it flies, it bursts. From Sally to Sandy,
to Sara, from Amy and Amy to Annie, to Ariel,

Deborah, Devorah, wave after wave after wave,
I see joyous throngs — there's Rachel, and Hara, Jen,
Jamie, Jessica, Jan, and Kara. There's Sharon, and Sharon,
and Sharon! Too many to name — we're just getting started!
For so long, the world was unimaginable with you in it,

now, we cannot imagine a world without you.
We bless the work of your hands, we bless
the work of your hearts. We are blessed, to be here,
still, just at the beginning.

The Pioneers Who Paved the Way

PAMELA S. NADELL, PhD

ON FOUNDERS' DAY 2022, as the Reform Movement gathered to recall the giants of the past, Rabbi Andrea Weiss, PhD, provost of Hebrew Union College–Jewish Institute of Religion, ascended the bimah. Reeling from the painful reports disclosing abuses of power and privilege committed by some of those men, she refused to read the list of yahrzeits usually recalled on this day.

Instead, she recited the names of four women who, in the 1920s and 1930s, sought ordination and whose stories I had told in my book *Women Who Would Be Rabbis*. Martha Neumark (Montor) at Hebrew Union College and Irma Levy Lindheim, Dora Askowith, and Helen Levinthal (Lyons) at the Jewish Institute of Religion failed then to convince the Reform Movement to ordain them rabbis.

In those years when feminist aspirations went unfulfilled all across the nation, their training prepared them not for rabbinical leadership but for sharing with women and children the Jewish knowledge they had acquired. After seven and a half years in rabbinical school, Martha Neumark Montor received a certificate qualifying her as a Sunday school principal. Irma Levy Lindheim would become Hadassah's national president. Dr. Dora Askowith, who already held a PhD, a rare accomplishment for any woman back then, taught history, including Jewish history, at Hunter, New York's free public college for women. Although the press showered attention on Helen Levinthal at her graduation for being as close to a rabbi as a woman could be, her future roles were those of wife, mother, and Jewish communal volunteer.

How fitting on Founders' Day to lift up these pioneers who paved the way to today, when we mark a half century of women in the rabbinate.

What We Have Learned

RABBI SANDY EISENBERG SASSO

IN THE EARLY 1970s, while I was in seminary and simultaneously pursuing a graduate degree, I proposed writing a dissertation on women in Judaism. I was advised that would be a mistake and was counseled to write about something "important"! As we celebrate fifty years of women in the rabbinate, I want people to know that it wasn't all that long ago when women's voices, narratives, and questions were discounted. It is easy to take the advances of the last years for granted. We must remain ever vigilant, vociferous, and visionary.

Two Jewish folktales ("Skotsl Kumt" and "Haberes Buenos") tell stories of women wanting to change their inferior status. In the Yiddish version, a human ladder is formed, and a single woman on the top is dispatched to inquire about the problem. In the Sephardic tale, a bird is sent. Neither the woman nor the bird returns.

We have learned two things over the last half century. First, while all of us are necessary, no one of us is sufficient. Having been on the periphery, we sought to include the margins. Second, circles are stronger than ladders. The revolutionary changes in ritual, theology, leadership, prayer, history, and community happened because of strong coalitions and powerful sisterhood. We left Jacob alone struggling with the angel at the Jabbok, and we crossed the river to reside with the women on the other side. There, in encounters with others, we found community and a life of the spirit that had long been silent.

Because I Am a Woman

Rabbi Ellen Weinberg Dreyfus

Back in the 1970s, when people heard that I was a rabbinical student, they would say to my mother, "She's going to be a WOMAN rabbi??" My mother would respond, "I don't know what other kind she could be." My mother's answer had greater wisdom than she realized at the time. Although I bristled at the idea of being a rabbi with an adjective and wanted to be just a rabbi among rabbis, I have come to realize that being a woman is more than an essential part of who I am and what kind of rabbi I became. I am the rabbi I am *because* I am a woman.

Being in the first generation of women to be rabbis had its advantages and its annoyances. Some doors were opened to me as the "first woman" in various settings. I also faced discrimination and bias, including congregations that, shall we say, declined the honor of interviewing me. I generally thought of it as their loss, but it still hurt. Like so many other women, I was mansplained, interrupted, and suffered microaggressions from both laypeople and male colleagues. But I decided early on that I didn't need to carry all that negativity with me, because I was too busy doing my work and being a mom and living my life. I am grateful for a supportive husband, a wonderful family, and a large circle of friends and colleagues who keep me going.

Women Rabbis

PHILIP SCHULTZ

To Rabbi Debra Stein

At the Big Shul on Rauber Street Grandma argued
in Yiddish with the angels floating around the purple
peeling ceiling about whether God was a woman.
Below, Dad sat with the other men, silently worrying.
Once I asked Grandma why women weren't rabbis
and the blue light in her eyes shined right through me.
Men, she said were afraid of women because women
knew where all their dreams were buried, and where
to hide after men blew up the world again. So now,
all these years later, I'm sitting downstairs with both
men and women, listening to a woman Rabbi welcome
in the New Year, remembering Grandma quoting from
the Talmud: *Be careful if you make a woman cry, God
counts her tears. The Woman came out of a man's rib,
not from his feet to be walked on . . . but from the side
to be equal. And next to the heart to be loved.* Okay,
Grandma's right, some things change for the better,
and now if you look up, you'll see her up in the balcony,
still arguing about how life and death are set before us
like delicacies in a kosher deli we must choose between.
Choose life, Grandma hollers down at me, however bitter
and capricious your misdeeds, humble and exalted
your prayers, history is a mother who alone knows
the recipe for happiness, devotion, and lokshen kugel.

A Profound Journey

Rabbi Mindy Avra Portnoy

Timing controls so many of life's decisions.

I was born in an era (1951) when multiple new possibilities (personal and professional) became open to women. My first experience of this change (albeit with limits) was my bat mitzvah ceremony, in my Conservative shul, on a Friday night. Even though there was no reading from the Torah scroll at that service, I was the first girl allowed to chant the *maftir* portion (albeit from a book). One small, yet significant step.

In 1969, Yale University decided to accept women undergraduates for the first time. I added one more application to my already finished (pre-computer) pile of papers.

And in 1972, during my junior year abroad in Israel, not yet sure of my career direction, but knowing that the choice would involve the study of Judaism, my mother sent me an article about Sally Priesand, about to be ordained as a rabbi. My life's path was becoming even more clear.

Fifty years later, I have served as a Hillel rabbi and congregational rabbi, a children's book author, a teacher, a pastoral counselor, a sermonizer, and a storyteller.

We women who are rabbis are still here, not only because doors and campuses and sanctuaries opened for us (my first published book was *Ima on the Bima: My Mommy Is a Rabbi*), but also because we took advantage of the opportunities as well as the challenges, paving the way for others to follow.

It has been a profound journey, for each of us and for the Jewish people.

Changed for the Better

Rabbi Jacqueline Koch Ellenson

For me, the opportunity of the past fifty years has been both personal and communal. In my own life, I was able to create my rabbinic path in an idiosyncratic way that matched my skills and interests and freed me from the perceived demands and constraints of congregational life. In the absence of role models, I was trying to figure out how to live a meaningful life—how to be a rabbi, how to be a wife and mother, and how to balance my personal and professional commitments. I had no idea that I was creating a reality for anyone beyond myself. I wasn't thinking then about how future women rabbis would construct their lives. But over time, I have come to see that these early efforts by myself and other women who were ordained in the first decade after Sally's ordination laid down tracks for women rabbis of the future. As we figured out how to live our lives as rabbis, we also helped others imagine how they would live their lives as rabbis. We had to be creative and, at times, confrontational as we broke norms and redefined roles. I now feel a sense of pride knowing that the norms we broke and those we created have helped all rabbis, regardless of gender, live more integrated, productive, and meaningful lives. The options we searched for personally are now validated and honored as rabbinic paths. Did we know when we started that we were going to change the rabbinate for the better? I'd like to think we did, and I know now that by creating various entryways to professional leadership, we did just that. We changed Jewish life, as well as the rabbinate, for the better.

A Legitimate Rabbi

RABBI PATRICE HELLER, PhD

I HAD BEEN ADAMANT about identifying as a "rabbi" without the qualifier of "woman" when I began my career in 1981 at Rodeph Shalom in Philadelphia, Pennsylvania. I wanted to be seen and accepted as a "legitimate" rabbi despite the continued focus on my hair.

Five years later I began my doctoral psychology studies at Bryn Mawr College and became an "interim" rabbi at various congregations. My six months leading the warm and welcoming Temple Shalom in Broomall, Pennsylvania was a powerful and joyous experience. Mayer Selekman was the charismatic and beloved rabbi of Temple Shalom, and I knew I could not fill his shoes. But what I did have that he did not was being a woman! Reclaiming being a "woman rabbi" became an opening to rich opportunities for creative change.

The congregation willingly joined me in this adventurous experiment. First, gender-neutral language was essential, and our minds, hearts, services, and ceremonies were transformed. I began a women's spirituality group, which continues to this day, thirty years later! I initiated adult b'nei/b'not mitzvah; four women enthusiastically commenced preparations.

Our final Shabbat eve was a jubilant celebration of women claiming their voices and place. Twin girls became b'not mitvah, four women were b'not mitzvah pioneers, the president and fabulous cantor ... all women. Then there was the woman rabbi, pregnant with her first child, a daughter.

I realize that I am not a rabbi who "happens to be a woman." With knowing clarity I fully embrace being a rabbi... *because* I am a woman.

The Most Revolutionary Contribution to American Jewry

Rabbi Amy R. Perlin, DD

THE MOST REVOLUTIONARY contribution to American Jewry in the twentieth century was HUC-JIR's decision to ordain Rabbi Sally J. Priesand in 1972. Since that time, HUC-JIR has ordained 839 women rabbis in America and Israel, with numbers increasing steadily every year.

Each one of HUC-JIR's women graduates has written a living history of transformative Judaism as they have been exemplars of Torah, groundbreaking leadership, and Jewish values in all walks of rabbinic life from the congregation to chaplaincy, military service to the world of scholarship. Rabbi Priesand "opened the door," as she is fond of saying, and she has proudly "held the door open," as she said to me just the other day. Those of us who followed her are eternally grateful for her courage, tenacity, and generosity of spirit.

As a 1982 rabbinic graduate of HUC-JIR and a member of the HUC-JIR Board of Governors, I am inspired every day by my fellow graduates who have navigated their communities through the COVID pandemic and are actively responding to the rapidly changing Jewish landscape of the twenty-first century. I am encouraged by a new generation of women committed to equity, inclusion, and institutional accountability. May we go from strength to strength, honoring our past, investing in our present, and visioning for our future.

Bar Mitzvah

Jehanne Dubrow

There was no other story in my childhood
but the one of a pencil point pressed
when he was thirteen in my father's palm.
Each time the words folded over
in their jagged cantillation, the rabbi dug
the lead deeper to inscribe the chanting there.
It's why I don't believe, my father told me
so many afternoons. On those days,
we sipped the sharpness of sugar crystals
with our tea. He read aloud from a novel,
often falling asleep at the kitchen table,
the book an open burden in his hands.
I would touch his arm to wake him—
Daddy, I would say, we're on the next page.
After his bar mitzvah, he didn't return
to a synagogue for forty years. Only
the new cut a surgeon made in his body
persuaded my father to sit again
in the doubtful light of a Friday evening.
Learning, he had learned, should hurt
beneath the skin. He learned this from cancer.
He learned this earlier from a man
called a rabbi. What could I say at the table,
in those distant days when I was a girl?

Now I want to be the teacher who erases
the pain from his palm. It's only a smudge,
I might say. It's the blessing of crumpled paper
or of writing over what was there before.
We could sit at the table and practice
Hebrew words together, how they almost
crumble like honey cake on the tongue.

These Fifty Years

RABBI AMY EILBERG, DMin

I COULD EASILY make the case that the world is more broken than it was fifty years ago, when Sally J. Priesand was ordained, or thirty-seven years ago, when I was ordained. A quick look at the news on any day of the week inundates us with stories of war, hatred, and injustice. It is not hard to find reasons for despair.

But our tradition teaches us to cultivate awareness of blessings. So, on this anniversary of the ordination of women, my thoughts are drawn to the ways in which the journey toward human dignity for all people has, in fact, progressed in these years. Surely, there is so much work to be done. But the cause of women's equality has advanced dramatically in these decades. The movement for women's liberation, in turn, encouraged the unfolding of liberation movements for other groups of people whose plight had been completely unrecognized. Today, we work for the dignity and empowerment of LGBTQ people. Gay marriage is the law of the land, and there are increasing protections for trans people. We are witness to a new stage in liberation work for BIPOC (Black, Indigenous, and People of Color) communities. We are coming to understand that inclusion refers not only to women and men, but to people of all gender identities and gender expressions. Many are beginning to recognize the stumbling blocks placed before those with physical and mental disabilities. In all of these ways, though the fight for rights continues, we have lived to see great progress in the march toward full human dignity for all people, and for this I am grateful.

L'dor Vador, Muckwanago, Wisconsin, 1994

CARLY SACHS

For Rabbi Carrie Carter

I could not name it then,
the year Mrs. Rotar let me play the King in *Alice in Wonderland*,
the summer Rabbi Carrie let me hold up the Torah.
My arms taking root under the canopy of words
whose sounds I knew,
but whose meaning I did not.

Back home it was my grandfather who wore the tallis,
got called to the Torah for an *aliyah*,
while my grandma slipped me hard candy
from her purse to keep me quiet as the Torah came by
and all the women held out their prayer books,
then brought them silently to their lips.

Rabbi Carrie told me to bend my knees
and breathe. I *trust you*, she said to me
that summer of 1994 at B'nai B'rith Beber Camp.

And it is Rabbi Carrie who I think of now in the kitchen
when I pass the challah dough to my daughter Ruthie
so she can feel its heft
and stickiness in her own hands,
something she can make
and mold how she sees fit.

And it is Rabbi Carrie whose voice comes back to me
when Ruthie runs up and down the steps and dances on the bimah
in the empty sanctuary at Temple Adath Israel
where I work.

It's yours and has always been yours
said Rabbi Carrie as the sweat soaked my pink polo shirt
and I took a step forward to balance the weight of everything unsaid,
everything I was holding,
known and not,
the sunlight and a girl holding a parchment etched with promises
that she would eventually hand to her own daughter.

Stepping into History

RABBI RICHARD F. ADDRESS, DMin

IN JUNE OF 1972, as we emerged from our ordination service at Plum Street Temple in Cincinnati, none of us could have imagined that we were stepping into history. Yes, Sally was part of our class and we knew this was historic, but what we did not know was that we were present at the beginning of a revolution.

Our rabbinate has, in so many ways, been shaped by the transformation that began on that day of ordination. There is no doubt that the impact of women in the rabbinate has restructured, reshaped, and reformed much of Judaism across the global denominational and institutional landscape.

I believe that this revolution was also part of a larger shift in how contemporary Jewish life has been lived. I believe the currents of change that began in 1972 helped pave the paths for the inclusion and openness to the LGBTQ community and the spiritual-worship changes that have become part of what we see now as normative.

Yes, there have been many benefits of this revolution. I have had the honor of working with many of my women colleagues in both pulpit and institutional worlds. There is also much still to be done, from equality in pay to a greater sensitivity to challenges in managing one's family with rabbinic and cantorial challenges.

There is no way we could have predicted what these fifty years would bring. In looking backward, we can take a measure of pride in being part of these expanding paths to Jewish life, and in looking forward, we hope that the positive progress will continue.

Good Enough

RABBI LEAH KROLL

THERE WERE SO FEW OF US at the beginning of this "experiment" of ordaining women and sending them (us) out into the North American Jewish community with the assumption that those communities were ready for us. Due to this, I felt great pressure to excel in everything I did lest my shortcomings would lead to the end of women rabbis. I carried this heavy weight on my shoulders for most of the 1980s. I worried that a mistake in chanting Torah or delivering just a so-so sermon would lead those in power to say, "See, women aren't astute enough to master chanting Torah and doing a simultaneous translation of it, and they are not smart enough to share a coherent and thoughtful sermon, interspersed with Jewish texts. They're too emotional."

My antidote to the fear of failing was *preparation*. I prepared and prepared and prepared—I overprepared for every task so that I could "show them" that an investment in women in the rabbinate would pay off in terms of new members, heightened participation from women in the community, and a greater engagement of our youth. This, too, was a burden that I felt. No matter how much I prepared, I worried if I would "be good enough" and if I would advance the status of women in the rabbinate or lead to its downfall.

There are so many of us now that we're a reality, and I no longer need to carry that heavy burden. My shoulders and my heart feel much lighter.

A New Jewish Narrative

Rabbi David Ellenson

THE DECISION TO ORDAIN WOMEN as rabbis matters because the patriarchal structure upon which Judaism was built and that remained hegemonic for millennia was correctly seen as no longer morally satisfactory. By extending rabbinical ordination to women, a process was begun that allowed Jewish women and men to understand that the exclusion of half our population from positions of authority in the public life of the Jewish people was inherently unethical, for it denied the full personhood of women. Women and men came to realize that a Judaism that did not allow the voices of women to be heard in communal discussions and that did not affirm the full dignity of women as persons was simply morally intolerable, and this realization facilitated the judgment that extended *s'michah* to women.

The decision to ordain women as rabbis has not resolved all the inequity of the past. However, that decision has ushered in a new era and initiated a process that allows for a new Jewish narrative to emerge, one in which gender justice can be realized and in which all people can participate as equals. There is yet a long way to go for the full promise of this journey of justice to be attained. However, the journey has begun, and that grants all of us cause for rejoicing. May this journey find ever-evolving fulfillment in the days ahead!

The Greatest Legacy of Fifty Years

JONATHAN D. SARNA, PhD

I STAND AMONG the first people in all of Jewish history who can proudly boast to have watched the ordination of my wife and my daughter.

Today, Ruth and Leah spend long hours surrounded by Jewish books. They study Torah (sometimes even with one another) and they teach Torah. Students—women and men, Jews and non-Jews—flock to their classes and lectures.

That, to my mind, is the greatest legacy of fifty years of women in the rabbinate. It has empowered the female half of the Jewish world to feel that Jewish learning—Torah in its broadest sense—belongs to them too. It is theirs to study and write and love and transmit.

The empowerment of women—their books, articles, lectures, sermons, and podcasts; those whom they inspire and teach; their students, their daughters, and all the learned Jewish women who follow in their footsteps—will be remembered as my generation's greatest single contribution to Jewish life and continuity.

The Shekhinah as Amnesiac
[What every woman rabbi secretly knows]

ALICIA SUSKIN OSTRIKER

> I was set up from everlasting, from the beginning
> before the earth was.... When he prepared the heavens
> I was there ... rejoicing always before him.
> —PROVERBS 8:23–30

then humanity named you wisdom
monarchs ruled according to your counsel
you prepared a table from which we ate

you were above rubies
and exalted like the palm tree
or like the rose bushes in Jericho

come on, surely by now you remember who you are
you're my mother my sisters my daughter
you're me

We will have to struggle so hard
to birth you
this time

the brain like a cervix

Our Spiritual Lineage

Rabbi Jill Hammer, PhD

As a woman rabbi, I cherish the role models I can look to from history and recognize that spiritual leadership is not a new role for women but a very old one. From rabbinical scholar Asnat Barzani of sixteenth-century Kurdistan to Ceti, the rabbess of fourteenth-century Zaragoza, from Aidel, daughter of the Baal Shem Tov, who acted as a rebbe and gave blessings, to Urania, chief of the synagogue singers in fourteenth-century Worms, to Regina Jonas of twentieth-century Berlin, we see examples of women doing rabbinic work and providing spiritual leadership prior to the ordinations that have occurred in recent generations. Bernadette Brooten's work to uncover titles among Jewish women in the first, second, and third centuries CE, such as "elder," "head of synagogue," and "priestess," in lands from Rome to Egypt to Israel, suggests this legacy extends deeply into the Jewish past and even farther back to the prophets Miriam and Deborah.

As I live out my own rabbinate, I find myself strengthened by the presence of these ancestors in the background. Coming from a sense of the antiquity of my role, not only as a rabbi carrying on the rabbinic journey, but as a woman doing the work of spirit, gives me a sense of grounding, responsibility, and purpose, and I try to convey that sense to others whom I teach and serve. To me, it feels important for all kinds of Jews, of all genders and walks of life, to have a feeling of spiritual lineage.

Eighty-Seven Years, Not Fifty!

Rabbi Dalia Marx, PhD

Regina Jonas (1902–1944), the first woman to become a rabbi, was a tragic pioneer. This German Jew of traditional background was ordained in December 1935 in Nazi Germany. At that time many rabbis left the country, and the need for spiritual guidance was great. She worked in several liberal communities and Jewish institutions. In 1942 she was deported to Theresienstadt, where she continued her rabbinic and educational work and served as *Seelsorgerin* (spiritual counselor) for her incarcerated fellow Jews, providing them with meaning and consolation. In October 1944 she was sent to Auschwitz and murdered there.

The story of Jonas was almost forgotten, until Katharina von Kellenbach, a Protestant theologian, found an ordinary-looking envelope in the central archive of the Jewish community after the unification of West and East Germany in 1990. In it were some photos of Jonas, her ordination certificate, and her thesis, in which she proved, based on the Rabbinic literature, that there is no halachic prohibition to ordain women as rabbis.

Regina Jonas was a tragic heroine not only because of her violent death, but also because she was forgotten. It is hard to explain why the Holocaust survivors who knew her and her uniqueness and who worked with her did not make sure that she is remembered. Many ponder today about the reasons for this "public amnesia." It took thirty-seven more years until the next woman, Sally Priesand, was ordained!

In recent years, efforts are being made to commemorate her. I am grateful for the opportunity to celebrate her life here, too.

Hungry God Touch

Devon A. Spier

A woman rabbinical student recalls a passage from one of
Rabbi Regina Jonas's last sermons.

i simply put could not find my self
in the chattery study halls
or stiff sanctuaries
of bearded Jewish men
their words
in final inked letters
set me off
so Off off
i went
stumbling
for you
for a beginning
landed at the gate of Auschwitz
there you greet me
bone disguised skin
your spectre
spelling out the words
love kindly
become a nation of blessing
humble selfless God love upon all of God's creation!
Your end
this nation
and you
starving hungry God woman

pillar of fire
pillar of smoke
wisdom cloud rising!
re-membering history
reshaping our being
becoming satisfied Hungry writing
God!

The First

Rabbi Bruce S. Block

"Do you know that young woman—you know—the one who wants to be a rabbi?" The questioner was one of the members of the adult study group at my student pulpit in Marion, Indiana, in 1969. "Sally Priesand," I replied. "Yes. I know her." Sally was three years behind me at HUC-JIR in Cincinnati. The questioner continued, "Well, could you invite her to come speak to us?"

When I returned to campus I met with Sally and asked her if she would come. Since the group met in private homes on Saturday evenings on the weekends I was there, she could ride with me, and the congregation would provide lodging, meals, and an honorarium. Sally told me she would be glad to come, provided that she lead the Shabbat service on Friday evening. That way, on Saturday evening, the group would be able to talk about the experience of having seen a woman as rabbi rather than merely discussing the idea of a woman as rabbi. I agreed, and so did the temple president, whose wife had asked the question that had led to inviting Sally.

Sally led the Shabbat evening service that Friday evening. The entire adult study group was present. The next evening, at the home of the temple president and his wife, Sally led the entire discussion. It was an intimate setting—a small group in a private home. And Sally Priesand, then a second-year rabbinical student, was a master teacher. She had taught by example, both on the bimah and in the skillful way she led the discussion. It was a first for those adults those evenings in the early spring of 1969 in Marion, Indiana. And all these years later, I have come to recognize the wisdom Sally had already possessed in gently setting a precondition: that she lead the Shabbat evening service that Friday in 1969.

Three years later, in 1972, Sally Priesand was ordained as a rabbi in Cincinnati's historic Plum Street Temple. She was the first. And other women would follow.

Women Rabbis

JUDITH KERMAN

Our family were atheists.
When I sat in synagogue for someone's
bar mitzvah, bearded men wearing shawls
stood at the front of the room,
bowing, chanting words I could not understand
from books I could not read.
The idea of women rabbis
never crossed my mind.

I never could be the kind of girl
they said I had to be
to attract men. If I'd been Catholic,
at least I could have been a nun.

Finally bat mitzvah at fifty, I painted
silk tallises, the shawls women never wore
at those bar mitzvahs — a night sky full of stars,
with dusk and dawn at either end, inscribed
"in beauty and glory You garb yourself."
I thought about becoming a rabbi,
reaching out to the fraying edges,
all those other Jews who've never found
a Judaism they can live with.

A Woman Rabbi Stands on Many Shoulders

RABBI ELLEN LIPPMANN

I AM A WOMAN RABBI because my grandparents worked with Rabbi Mordechai Kaplan to start a new kind of shul that became the flagship of the Reconstructionist Movement.

I am a woman rabbi because my parents made Jewish home ritual joyous and services at our Reform temple a regular part of every week.

I am a woman rabbi because Jewish women like Gloria Steinem showed my generation what women's liberation could look like.

I am a woman rabbi because the month I graduated from college, Sally Priesand was ordained and every type of media of the time exploded with the news.

I am a woman rabbi because Rabbi Mike Robinson drew me into Shabbat Torah study after swim practice and asked me to speak about Jonah one Yom Kippur.

I am a woman rabbi because coming out as a lesbian led me to come out in all the parts of my identity and Jewish was a big part.

I am a woman rabbi because my wife supported my study and my community-building and my social activism at every turn.

I am a woman rabbi because the nearly-all-male faculty of HUC-JIR saw fit to ordain me.

I am a woman rabbi because the members of the community I founded and led saw me as rabbi and offered support and respect in all the ways that mattered.

No woman rabbi gets there alone. No marginalized person achieves alone. Each of us stands on the shoulders of those who came before and those who held us up and those who inspired us and those who opened doors so we could walk through. To each and every person who did that for me, I offer gratitude and honor. Your efforts joined mine to make me a woman rabbi.

The Expansion of "Rabbi"

RABBI SHIRA STERN, DMin, BCC

FOR MILLENNIA, the definition of the rabbinic role was confined to the pulpit, the *beit din*, or the classroom. While the twentieth century added social activism to the mix, it is only in the last fifty years that we have reimagined what choices are now available to clergy. I believe that expansion of what rabbis do has been in large part due to the influx of women into our seminaries.

Creating meaningful expressions that enhance Jewish connection has moved our leaders out of the sanctuary and into the communities we serve. Women have shown by necessity and by example that conforming to past standards does not work for everyone and that transformation for some leaders can reshape the way our people see *themselves* and *their* role in making Judaism thrive.

Women have taken *amcha* beyond brick and mortar where prayer and study were confined. Women have legitimized options for prayer that include spiritual hiking, meeting in community venues that change every week, and having retreats in centers that include new spiritual activities like yoga and Eastern-style meditation. And a growing number of women rabbis have chosen to serve at the bedside, in long-term care facilities, in prisons, and in disasters, elevating the act of chaplaincy to a sacred art. That has been my *kavanah* and my purpose, offering comfort to patients and teaching others to do the same. This work has enriched my life immeasurably, and I am grateful to the women who have taught me to find holy places outside the box.

Spiritual Vision

Rabbi Elyse D. Frishman

Perhaps one advantage to being an early woman rabbi was that the rabbinic role could be reimagined. I was brought into the congregation to be terrific with children and teens. It was only when adults realized that Jewish learning and living began with them—not me—that our true work began.

Together, congregants and I wove a spiritual vision and leadership: a collaborative *b'rit* based on respect, vulnerability, and deliberate commitment to *adult* learning and worship to inspire and reinforce Jewish living outside synagogue walls.

K'hilah k'doshah blossoms from a balance of *chesed* and *g'vurah*, of compassion and boundary, of love and limits. Sacred community assumes inclusivity, the deep recognition of the other. We could disagree *because* we agreed to play nicely. No parking lot gossip. Committee meetings opened with a reading of our vision, mission, and core values. We upheld diverse opinions grounded in commitment to our shared vision. We devoted ourselves to managing conflict with as little rancor as possible.

We studied together. We prayed together. We wrestled and comforted and grew together.

And that is a love story.

Reform Judaism, 1960s, Long Island

JESSICA GREENBAUM

We generally sat many rows back and I could tell my parents felt
happiest there—my brothers running in the hallways, and me
turning the wedding ring on my mother's soft hand. She so loved
me there. A woman lit the candles and was gone. The cantor's voice
drilled out of the earth and the rabbi in his black robe brought
Dracula to mind. As the men went on I considered
my shoe buckle, divided the rows of wooden rafters by two
then three. Was custom, at heart, about boredom? Or more sneakily—
obedience? The Sunday school teachers those years—uncles
from another planet—handed out Israeli newspapers and tested
our endurance for abstractions until, on Sunday mornings
while my family slept, I took my allowance and left the house
made a stop at the luncheonette, then sat on a hillside and ate
candy till midday, school over. Yet, as planned by the ancestors
here I am because the Hebrew and music filtered into the dirt of me
and the field of my spirit was harrowed for that season when
the women's words fall there. Often I've wondered who I might
have been had our stories of departures, manna, and rebellion
found me as a girl. But that's like asking who we would have become
had we blasted out the black-and-white fire unscathed. I'll never
know. It's a burn field, these burn marks my first true teachers.

Telling Our Stories

Rabbi Ellen Lewis

FROM THE TIME we were just students, we—the early women—were asked to tell our stories. That request came from many quarters. It presented a challenge because we were at the very beginning of our stories. We had yet to have stories to tell. All these years later, now that we have stories to tell, the challenge is a different one: which stories are worth sharing and why. Yes, there were funny stories, and yes, there were difficult stories, and yes, there were even terrible stories. But is there a purpose in telling a story simply for the sake of the telling of a story?

I think of how the stories told by our ancestors were redacted with purpose in mind. Those early editors intentionally shaped the story of the Jewish people so that we would inherit not just a story but a story with particular meaning. What meaning would I want my story to convey to future generations? I would want them to know that, yes, there were hard parts, but that I can talk about the hard parts without reliving the pain. I would want them to know that while those stories have led me to the place where I am today, those old narratives have no claim on me. I can tell my personal story today with a sense of satisfaction and liberation, having moved on from the past to a fulfilling and meaningful rabbinate.

I'll Show You

Rabbi Lisa A. Edwards, PhD

"OH YEAH? I'LL SHOW YOU." Had you known me as a child, you would have been surprised to hear me say such a thing. But say it I did, albeit to myself, when a religious school teacher told our class, "Women can't be rabbis."

Lucky for me, I wasn't quite old enough to be the first. I remain grateful to the women who preceded me. When I actually applied (twenty-five years later), I had yet to meet a woman rabbi or even see one on the bimah. Living in Iowa City, Iowa brought me out as a Jew and as a lesbian, but when I dreamed up the idea of a lesbian and gay synagogue (the other letters came later—B, T, Q, I, A+), I was so sheltered from the coasts that I didn't yet know such places already existed.

However, I had my share of firsts: turning up at HUC-JIR's Jerusalem campus with a woman partner two years before an open admissions policy, coming out at first interviews for congregational positions in the first class with openly lesbian rabbinical students, serving twenty-five years as the rabbi at the world's original gay and lesbian synagogue (Beth Chayim Chadashim in Los Angeles, founded in 1972). Could I have done any of that if women hadn't braved those spaces before me? Maybe, but I am thankful to have run the gauntlets I did with their guidance, presence, influence, and friendship.

Had There Been a Woman

ROBIN BECKER

For Sally Greenberg

Had I heard a woman's voice
chanting the sacred
Dayeinu

Had there been a woman
at the bimah wearing a tallit
Dayeinu

Had she carried the Torah
up and down the center aisle
of the synagogue
Dayeinu
as women and men leaned in touching
the silken cover

Had she an office where I could confide
my fears my shame
Dayeinu
seek her counsel in safety

How many of us might have
felt worthy
Dayeinu

had a woman scholar rabbi celebrant
welcomed us into the texts
as vital and necessary

interpreters of law and narrative
Dayeinu
How can we but honor those
who persisted

without encouragement but with faith
in themselves
Dayeinu
and in a Judaism

of deliberative compassionate
women's minds
Dayeinu

Had there been a woman rabbi
at the hospital at the gravesite
Dayeinu

we might have taken a seat
at the head of the seder table

where today Sally says the *Kiddush*
washes her hands blesses the parsley
dipping it into the tears
Dayeinu
of our enslavement

Liberation

RABBI JANET ROSS MARDER

And after it rains there's a rainbow and all of the colors are black.
It's not that the colors aren't there—it's just imagination they lack.
Everything's the same back in my little town.
                              —"My Little Town," Paul Simon (1975)

PAUL SIMON's lyrics evoke a claustrophobic community, a place you can't wait to get out of. I've read that the song is based on a real place—one of those dying industrial towns where the economy is stagnating, young people are strangled by lack of opportunity, and a pall of air pollution darkens everything you see. But for me that little town has always represented a state of mind as well. It's a place of limited horizons, meager choices, and little scope for hope.

For far too long, little girls have grown up confined in little towns of the mind, hemmed in and held back by a dearth of possibilities for their future. Lack of imagination chokes the human spirit, depriving you of the chance to envision a different life, express your gifts, discover who you could become. And when girls live in constricting environments, it is not only girls who suffer. The world is impoverished, deprived of the gifts of half the population.

The opening of the rabbinate to women fifty years ago, along with the opening of other professions, was an act of human liberation. And liberation—even an imperfect, incomplete liberation—is a profound blessing. I am grateful to have grown up in a time when I was free to choose a path that brought me deep fulfillment; grateful for all that my colleagues and I have been able to contribute as rabbis. The world is richer when all the colors in the rainbow shine forth.

Breaking Through Centuries of Constriction

Rabbi Julie Greenberg

In the early 1980s, I met my first woman rabbi, the night before my meeting with the Admissions Committee of the Reconstructionist Rabbinical College. As her golden haired one-year-old tugged at her legs, I saw a new model of the rabbinate, one that integrated nurturing and power.

My Jewish sisters and I were exploring what it meant to practice Jewish feminist leadership. What would it look like to challenge Jewish patriarchy with traditional and innovative Jewish women's folk practices?

During those years, I was also building a family as a member of the queer web. The Reconstructionist Rabbinical College considered me an "unwed mother." In that hostile environment, I wondered how I, a solo mom, would support my two-year-old and the second baby growing inside me.

The solidarity of sisterhood and liberation sustained me, even when I retreated to the rhododendrons in the arboretum across the street from the college for a cry. In that arboretum, I comforted the part of me that wanted to please my male teachers. Before I entered the college, I had enjoyed being recognized as a high achiever. It hurt me to be treated as marginal and less-than. I was a failed straight male rabbi.

Together and with allies and guides, we were transgressive and creative and prophetic and disruptive. We celebrated same-sex love and interfaith love and diverse family love, breaking through centuries of constriction. We insisted on childcare at every public event and on gender balance on every panel and program. And by seeing ourselves as a necessary face of Judaism, as voices of the future, we changed a slice of the world.

If God Could

JO-ANN MORT

If God could return all those years
when we sat outside or upstairs or behind
a barrier, when we shouted but no one heard,
when we prayed but our prayers were dismissed,
when the white silk of the tallit was kept
from our shoulders and we covered our arms
instead with our best jackets and dresses from Bonwit's.

We hugged our prayers to our hearts in silence.

If God could, but never mind.
We need no one's permission—not even God's.
The sanctuary is full of women and children.
The rabbi leads us—
our voices, loud and whispering.
Her voice, trilling with the empty decades.

O God of our fathers and mothers
O God of our sons and daughters
O God of our grandmothers, we gather
all the silenced voices in a circle.
The sanctuary is full like never before,
full with the union of every voice.

Ripple Effects

~::~

In one of my lives,

JUDY KATZ

I think I'd like to be a rabbi
but I'd have to change the word—it's too much
like a worn-out man's suit, a little dandruff on the collar.
It may be a classic cut, but it just wouldn't look good
on me. I'm not sure there is a word for the kind of *blank*
I'd want to be. I think it would have to incorporate artist
since "beautifying the commandments" is one of those things
I'm likely to take super seriously. And it would be good
if it could indicate both woman and friend, because I'd want
to dole out the kind of energy I get from my women friends—
like the other day in the park, when L. stopped to look at
the blooms on the redbud tree, spongy little nibs that grow
directly out of the branch, we were talking about how everything
in childrearing, it turns out, has to do with learning to let go,
which one has to do over and over, and how it was understood
that the conversation *and* the walk were all one thing.
Maybe the word I'm looking for needs to be a whole phrase:
The One Who Makes Anything You're Going Through Better,
for instance. That's the name I would have given Miriam,
the first woman rabbi I met and really got to know. It was right
before my wedding. We sat at her kitchen table in Brooklyn
and drank tea. She asked how O. and I had met, and what
my family was like growing up. She asked what I wanted
in a wedding ceremony. She wondered how I felt about the word

God. I felt fine. I felt whatever this person would bring
to the moment of my marriage, would add to it, make it richer
and more understandable to me. I knew that under the chuppah
she would slow things down; bring beauty and breaking
of glass, my mother's (invisible) presence and, if I wanted,
God's. And she was an artist and a woman and becoming
a friend. She would fill in every blank.

Changing the Fabric of Israeli Society

RABBI KINNERET SHIRYON

WHEN I ENTERED HUC-JIR in 1977, I began the first steps to fulfill my dream of becoming the first woman rabbi to function in the history of the State of Israel. My family, friends, and classmates warned me that I would be jumping from the frying pan into the fire. The concept of women rabbis was still very new—in Israel it was unheard of. I was ordained in 1981 and moved to Israel in 1983 with the desire to effect change in Israeli society. I succeeded despite the many obstacles I faced. I became a role model for other women. Today there are fifty women rabbis in Israel. My influence spread beyond just the liberal religious movements into the very fabric of Israeli society. Women rabbis have sensitized Israelis to the following:

- Egalitarian approaches in prayer settings
- Inclusive language and God language in liturgy
- Attentiveness to the gender-based nature of the Hebrew language, finding innovative ways of changing the way we communicate our values through language
- New models of religious leadership
- New ceremonies for marking life-cycle and pivotal events in women's lives as well as that of other previously unacknowledged members of the community
- Changes in teaching curriculum toward equality
- Raised consciousness in all the streams of religious and secular life to a more egalitarian society

It has been a privilege to lead this remarkable transformation.

Representing All the Others

RABBI NAAMAH KELMAN

IN 1992, SHORTLY AFTER I became the first woman rabbi to be ordained in Israel, I was a last-minute replacement on an interfaith mission to Japan. There were not a lot of Israelis involved in that crucial work then, and to be honest, my rabbinic resume was still (ahem) a bit thin. However, the organizers did promote me as the "first woman rabbi in Israel." At the beginning, I tried to explain that I was not the first, that I was following in Sally Priesand's footsteps, that there were other first women rabbis in the United States. Then I realized that in Tokyo, in the fall of 1992, I was *their* first woman rabbi, and I had better represent all the others who came before me! One Muslim delegate from Egypt, whose English was weak, did manage, with a smile, to tell me: No women imams ever!

A wonderful local Catholic nun explained to me that most men at the gathering could not fathom why I had left husband and children to come; there must be something wrong with me or my husband.

So now I was representing all women rabbis, all working mothers, all feminists. After this conference, I was invited to many international gatherings. Luckily, my late father, Rabbi Wolfe Kelman, had been the first generation of Liberal rabbis to engage in interfaith dialogue, and I took many mental notes at our family's Shabbat table, always watching him in action. He was and remains my most powerful rabbinic model.

Although I was expected to marry a rabbi or give birth to one, I did what Gloria Steinem told our generation to do—I became a rabbi.

The Unthinkable Became Imaginable

RABBI MICHAEL MARMUR, PhD

WHEN RABBI NAAMAH KELMAN was ordained by HUC-JIR in Jerusalem in 1992, the unthinkable became imaginable. Before then, many had believed that attitudes toward Judaism in Israel—"secular" as well as "religious"—would not allow for the possibility of women rabbis. The first Reform man had been ordained in Jerusalem a decade or so earlier, and some members of the Board of Overseers of the college believed that Israeli society was not ready for this precedent of ordaining women.

They were wrong. Thirty years later, women rabbis are to be found in Israel (and in many other places), transforming congregations and institutions, providing thought leadership and education at the highest level, promoting new approaches to civil discourse and Israel-Diaspora relations, offering breakthrough techniques in family dynamics and pastoral care, and active in many other fields. The impact of that historic moment in 1992, itself made possible by the pioneering moments that preceded it, extends beyond the Reform Movement. Groups across the denominational spectrum have been inspired by this precedent to make meaningful, irreversible change.

It was a privilege to be present on the day Rabbi Naamah Kelman made history back in 1992. It has been an even greater privilege to witness how she and the many who followed her have exploded myths and expanded horizons. In 1992, history was made. Every day since, it is being reimagined.

Called

Rabbi Karyn D. Kedar

When I was young, a dusty light from some faraway place
filled my inner being. It's like God came calling.

From then on, my life has been a tug of war.

To the right, obstinate world, demanding I abstain, pulling at
    my midnight fears,
dark whisperings — you can't, you shouldn't, how dare you!

To the left, unrelenting destiny, fearless, tugging with mag-
    netic force, saying,
Arise daughters of Israel. An uprising is at hand.

I've been fighting my entire life, embattled soul, and the
    Goddess of Splendor holds me still,
for I am wounded, tired, determined, indignant, magnificent,
    necessary. And she says,

Be bold.
Be brave.
Be beautiful.

I want only to serve.
In truth, that's all I've ever wanted.
To awaken that dust filled light within us all.
To affirm and animate the beauty of the world.
To heal what is broken, there is so much broken.
To practice faith and kindness and compassion.
To dispel despair. To teach hope and grace.
To shake the world of complacency.
To pray. To plead. To elevate.

To live with meaning
and purpose
and love.

Dear sisters of Israel, be bold, be brave, be beautiful.
We have been called. Splendid, glorious, dusty light.

Just Souls

RABBI PAULINE BEBE

Vayihyu v'einav k'yamim achadim b'ahavato otah.
—Genesis 29:20

ND THEY WERE in *his eyes like a few days, because of his love for her.* This beautiful verse about the elasticity of time shows us that time is relative, and when you are moved by passion, a long time can appear like a wink of an eye. Henri Troyat wrote, "Vocation is when your passion has become your mission." My time in the rabbinate is such that all the difficulties that I encountered more than thirty years ago—and some still today—have been effaced by the everyday gifts that my mission has brought to my heart and my life. Time has passed, but experience has taught me the ability to work better, by the side of people.

When I am asked whether, as a woman, I made a special contribution to the rabbinate, I am always embarrassed. I feel I am making my contribution as a rabbi, not as a woman or as a female rabbi. I believe people are just souls, whatever the shape of their body; a smile drawn on a sad face will always be a smile, and our mission as rabbis is to draw smiles on people's faces. They might be smiling and crying at the same time, but they will feel, with the help of the wisdom from our beautiful tradition, that they matter and that at that very moment, their lives are truly worth living.

Without the Pressure of Success

RABBI LEA MÜHLSTEIN

MY FAVORITE PIECE by the feminist art collective Guerrilla Girls is a 1988 work entitled *The Advantages of Being a Woman Artist.* The poster, words in a plain sans serif font in black printed on a white background, summarizes in thirteen short points the systemic biases against women in the art world. About five years ago, as part of an art exhibition that celebrated the political nature of Liberal Judaism, I created a new version of the poster entitled "The Advantages of Being a Woman Rabbi." While giving my version a specific Jewish clergy twist, I chose to retain the first point from the original version: "Working without the pressure of success." For me this encapsulates the experience of being a woman rabbi — even in 2023.

I look with great pride at the many women rabbis who have made and continue to make an incredible contribution to Jewish life and wider society. I have been blessed to stand on their shoulders, never experiencing the feeling that I am succeeding only despite my gender. And yet, to this day I notice that the success of women rabbis is still treated with a sense of surprise. Though I yearn for a time when the gender of the rabbi no longer influences our expectation of how successful they will be, in the meantime, fellow women rabbis, let's use this freedom to our advantage — for there are plenty of other additional pressures that weigh us down!

Just Rabbis

Rabbi Alona Lisitsa, PhD

I AM FIFTY YEARS OLD. This means that since I was born, women have been paving the road for me. I am grateful for this road; I feel blessed to walk on it.

I was born in Kyiv, Ukraine, and in the 1970s there, I could not have had the slightest idea about women rabbis and their struggles; being a Jew was enough of a challenge. You do not dream to become something you have never seen nor heard of.

While I was a rabbinical student at HUC-JIR in Jerusalem, I started to learn more about the firsts: the first woman rabbi ordained in Israel, the first sabra rabbi, the first Russian-speaking rabbi, and also the very first women ordained in the United States, in the United Kingdom, and in Europe; the first in the army, the first in the chaplaincy, the first *eim beit hadin* (the head of the rabbinic court), the first presidents of the CCAR and MARAM. Each one of them is a source of pride and admiration and a reason for celebration.

I belong to a generation of "just rabbis." We are not the firsts in anything—we walk the road paved for us. The women before me made it possible even for Israelis to say to women, "Ah, you're a rabbi? Fine." That does not mean there are no stumbling blocks unique to women on this road. Some remain, but the road is paved. For a woman, becoming a rabbi has turned into something more normal—one of the careers on the list a girl can consider. That form of heroism is now less and less on demand—women rabbis are now an integral part of Israeli social landscape. And I am happy not to be a hero. There is joy in being just normal.

Mother Psalm 6

Rabbi Rachel Barenblat

Don't chew on your mama's tefillin
I say, dislodging the leather
from your damp and eager grasp.
We play peekaboo beneath my tallit,
hiding your face and revealing it
the way God is sometimes present
sometimes not. You like the drums,
the fiddle and clarinet.
You bang your rattle on the floor.
As we sing "Praise God,
all you elders and young children"
you bellow and we laugh.
During silent prayer your yearning
opens my floodgates.
When the Torah is carried around
I waltz you in my arms, my own scroll.
All my prayers are written
in your open face.

Paying It Forward

RABBI DEBORAH KAHN-HARRIS, PhD

I TURNED FOUR in 1972. I cannot say that I remember a great deal about the ordination of women nor, hand on heart, did this have any impact on my young life. I was raised a Conservative Jew and had to fight every step of the way for the "basics"—a bat mitzvah on equal terms to my brothers, a tallit and t'fillin, reading from Torah. And despite a distant thought that I might like to be a rabbi someday, I couldn't imagine a world where that was possible. And then, when I finally met a woman rabbi in college, the axis of my world tilted, and her presence suddenly made my aspirations possible. Without her, without the women who forged ahead of me in rabbinical school, without the female colleagues who put up with the comments and the restrictions arbitrarily placed upon them and the pay inequalities and much else, I would not be where I am today. When I applied for my current role, I did not think about whether I was breaking some sort of barrier. I owe that to all the women in the rabbinate who precede me. That is a gift I endeavor each day to pay forward, to work to ensure that the next generation of colleagues—whatever their gender and sexuality—are free to give all of themselves to our sacred role without prejudice.

A New Learning Was Being Born

Rabbi Nancy H. Wiener, DMin

> *A new learning is about to be born.... It is a learning in reverse order. A learning that no longer starts from Torah and leads to life, but the other way around: from life to the Torah.*
> — Franz Rosenzweig

WITH THE SPIKE in women faculty and administrators (mid-1990s to early 2000s), a new learning was being born. A new, more holistic approach honoring each student for the unique individual they are—in their beauty and their messiness—impels curricular changes and a proliferation of opportunities for students to engage in reflection. Cooperation, interdependence, mutual growth, and personal *sh'leimut* now intentionally take place alongside deep, serious text study. The team effort of administrators, faculty, fieldwork mentors, faculty advisors, and spiritual directors contributes to and expands the vision of the formation of future clergy. While not solely driven by the women of HUC-JIR, our support and promotion of these commitments, both personally and professionally, have been central to this new learning taking root.

We now consciously articulate culture-changing messages, reflective of feminism, to our students:

> All you have—ultimately, ever—to offer others is your self. Get to know who you are so you can bring your best self to all that you do. Value reflection—so your past experience can lead to informed future decisions. Let others help you reflect and share their insights and understandings. Cooperation, not competition, is life-affirming and productive. Asking for and offering help is mutually beneficial. You never need to navigate difficulties and issues alone; you have a web of relationships and an ancient tradition to draw upon and support you. Internalizing and trying to live these truths will help you truly serve others.

Why I Didn't Become a Rabbi

Hila Ratzabi

Because I've heard too much about synagogue politics from my
mom who is ready to quit the board

Because the Earth is my synagogue, and God is wherever we call
Her/Them

Because I'm judgmental and impatient with others

Because I'm not much of a davener

Because I'm easily distracted in synagogue

Because I'm more interested in the white space in the margins of the
siddur

Because I can't pick a synagogue, so I go to three: Reform, Conservative, and Reconstructionist (and I keep trying to hang out with the
secular and Chabad folks, too)

Because my rabbis are both ordained and unordained, Jewish and
non-Jewish

Because I've edited so many other people's sermons I couldn't
believe in my own

Because I'm filled with both doubt and faith, and I never know
which one will show up

Because my non-Jewish atheist partner keeps telling me to go to
rabbinical school, and I don't want him to win that argument

Because who could hold all that life and death at once, births,
weddings, funerals, weekly, daily?

Because I can't pray on command

Because I still don't know how I feel about collective revelation or
revelation in general

Because every time I try to muster belief in our founding narrative,
I become suspicious of the patriarchy

Because I don't know if Judaism can really be feminist without
starting from scratch

Because visionaries like Etty Hillesum, Clarice Lispector, and Hélène
   Cixous were missing from my Jewish education
Because these women are my rabbis but transcend Jewish literary
   and spiritual categories
Because these women were their own religions
Because language cannot contain God
Because language must shatter like the vessels of Creation
Because I often can't find the words and don't know where to look
Because God is not involved in history and I'm okay with that
Because prophecy doesn't do TikTok and neither do I
Because I have faith in my rabbi friends and they're enough for me
Because I watch from the sidelines with my side-eye, relieved it's not
   me on the bimah
Because a poet can slip under the radar
Because I have a voice and I use it when I choose to
Because the path has been paved and I chose another
Because the path is still being paved and mine is bursting with weeds
Because the purple lupines in my garden have not instructed me
   otherwise
Because they said stay still, they said listen, they said you are right
   where you're supposed to be

Previously Unimaginable

Daphne Lazar Price

In 1972, the idea of Orthodox women clergy seemed out of reach. Then in 1997, I had two defining experiences.

First, I attended the First International Conference on Feminism and Orthodoxy. This 1000+ person gathering launched the Jewish Orthodox Feminist Alliance (JOFA), an organization I am now honored to lead.

Second, I participated in the Torat Miriam fellowship's inaugural cohort, spearheaded by Rabbis Avi Weiss and Saul Berman. Over ten months, ten rising Orthodox women leaders studied with American Orthodoxy's intelligentsia and taught in communal settings. Toward the program's end, we gathered to imagine what a second year or internship might look like—but at that time we could not imagine a pathway forward.

Even as my personal life was entrenched in the Orthodox community, prior to my JOFA role, my professional work brought me into close contact with a broad range of American and Israeli women rabbis. Their profound impact as clergy, teachers, and academics, preachers, t'filah leaders, and healing pastoral figures further clarified for me the potential and need for such leadership in Orthodox life.

Through JOFA, I am now engaged in efforts to expand spiritual, ritual, intellectual, and leadership opportunities for women within the framework of Jewish law, to create a vibrant and equitable Orthodox community. We do this by advocating for girls' and women's increased, meaningful ritual participation and by widening pathways toward leadership in synagogues, learning institutions, and Jewish communal organizations.

Today, the seeds JOFA planted are bearing fruit. Women are engaging more deeply in advanced halachic studies and earning pastoral, educational, and communal credentials. Indeed, clergy roles for Orthodox women have increased exponentially.

These women are positioned to break through glass ceilings, serving as Orthodox clergy in pulpits, schools, college campuses, and communal organizations in capacities previously unimaginable for Orthodox women.

Now, it's no longer a question of whether we can have Orthodox women as spiritual leaders, but rather "How can we not?"

What Moses Learned about Sinai in Akiva's Class

A Proposal and a Personal Memory

JUDITH BAUMEL

In honor of Rabbis Jackie, Larry, Roni,
and Dr. Jeremy Tabick at CSAIR

Suppose it's how we grow up. When she was called
to bless the Torah section, both her sons
and husband rose and stayed on foot, they stood
to celebrate the woman, rabbi, first.

They stood as elders circling Sinai's base
as if before them sapphire paving shone
from where she rose. It's what we knew
in our betrothal. Thunder, lightning, fire.

Suppose it's all of us who hear and see.
Each one of us reforming boundaries,
each going past the childish gendered space
and saying now's the time that we will do.

Suppose we've left the narrow place beneath
the wide high view that she has brought us to.

The Story Is Only Just Beginning

RABBA SARA HURWITZ

IN 2009, when I was ordained as the first female Orthodox rabbi to serve, I sought permission through halachic texts and the few women who created precedent and legitimacy for me. My role models were Devorah the Prophetess, Beruriah, and Hannah Rachel Verbermacher, the Maiden of Ludmir. I taught about Rabbi Bakshi Doron, the chief rabbi of Israel who, in 1993, ruled unequivocally that "women can be of the *g'dolim* [great leaders] of the generation and serve as halachic decisors" (*Responsa Binyan Av* 65:5). And of course, I stood on the shoulders of the women who had the courage to break the glass ceilings of their communities in the Reform, Conservative, and Reconstructionist Movements.

Today, the conversation is no longer about whether Orthodox women can be members of clergy. Today, women *are* rabbis. In just fourteen years, our sixty alumnae have added intrinsic value to the *beit midrash*, the bimah, the classroom, hospitals, and life-cycle events. Graduates of Yeshivat Maharat have impacted tens of thousands of Jews, teaching Torah in over fifty communities worldwide. The story of Orthodox women as rabbis is only just beginning to be written. I can only imagine how much better our world will be fifty years from now, with women from every denomination sitting at the table, shaping our communal conversations.

Normal, Extraordinary

BETH HUPPIN

I have learned much from my teachers, more from my colleagues,
but from my students, more than all the others.
— Babylonian Talmud, Taanit 7a

A FUNDAMENTAL SHIFT occurred in the 1960s when our small-town Conservative synagogue allowed girls to have bat mitzvah ceremonies, though limits to female participation continued. For example, by the year I became bat mitzvah in 1970, I chanted the haftarah words, but my father chanted the blessings. Normal synagogue life included women regularly attending Shabbat services, although the text within the Torah scroll remained off-limits to female chanting or viewing. I rarely saw adult women on the bimah except to light Shabbat candles.

Still, I loved Judaism and Jewish learning, so I became a Jewish educator, then the acceptable professional path for females in the Conservative Movement. While some of my feminist peers pushed for acceptance to rabbinical school and later became the first female Conservative rabbis, that option simply never occurred to me.

Fast-forward about thirty years. I'm teaching a fifth-grade day school class, reading aloud a story about a rabbi faced with a dilemma. An inquisitive eleven-year-old girl raises her hand. "When the rabbi made her decision, do you think that she . . ." I don't hear the end of the question. The words "her" and "she" stun me. This confident pre–bat mitzvah girl assumes that a generic "rabbi" in a story refers to a woman.

Normal for her. Extraordinary for me.

What She Loves

RABBI SONJA K. PILZ, PhD

My great-grandmother
Is an ancient woman of fifty years
On a yellow photograph
I know very little about her
Other than that
She had nine living children
And three who died during childbirth
I was told she tried
To get rid of the crib, playsuits, and wipes
Any number of times
And then just gave up.

My grandmother was her youngest
She did not marry well
But was very happy
During the days of her marriage
Polishing sowing and sewing
Plowing through the mud
She had two children
In spite of many doctors
And her eyes were shining
When she watched me
Cleaning up.

My mother, her youngest, was her family's first generation
She went straight ahead
To medical school
And ran a lab
I remember

When we were children
We used to hear
How she would always be working
"too much"
I played at her office
And looked at pictures of feet and cracks.

She came and stayed with us
Made me write down my hours
To tell me that now
It was me who was working
"too much"
She did not need to
As my husband had already told me
I hear it quite often
"spend more time with your family"
"go home"
"rest up."

I am due any day now
Waiting for her
Arriving
How many hours
Will be her
"too much"
I promise her silently
As I feel her moving
That I won't ever be counting the hours
During which she does
What she truly loves.

Role Model

Joy Ladin

My son is three, cheeks like flushed full moons, *kippah* of curls coppering his head, plush toy Torah scroll cradled to his chest. Was this before or after the terror? It doesn't matter. The lightning is sleeping in his brain, and he is playing what these days is his favorite game, rabbi, marching the Torah through his backyard synagogue, proclaiming to me, his congregation, mixing nonsense with *Sh'ma*, sky reflected in each brown iris, a burning bush in every syllable.

Now I see—this is what he is meant to be. The synagogue is his favorite place, he learned to walk by clambering onto the bimah, knowing the rabbi, Sheila Peltz Weinberg, will smile indulgently down on the fledgling generation she has inspired, the little amen, unshackled to the chain of patriarchs, unscarred by the scar left by the mohel with a tremor who circumcised him in an empty room in my reluctant arms. Knowing she will let him play at her feet. Invite him to open the ark.

He played that game for years. Baked challah every Friday for his college Hillel.

But now he's still three, chanting, shouting, Torah and sunlight radiating from each cheek. Suddenly his sermon stops. He's quiet, troubled, looking up for the answer on which he believes his life depends: "Does a rabbi *have* to be a woman?"

All the Answers and Excuses
in the World

TAMAR BIALA

Why do we need wise, courageous, creative women rabbis? So that we won't have to write such midrash as this one, penned by Rivkah Lubitch, an advocate for women in Israel's rabbinic courts.

THERE WAS A LITTLE GIRL who would pester her mother and ask, why do the males humiliate us, saying "Blessed is He who did not make me a woman"? And her mother would bring her all the answers and excuses in the world, and they didn't put her daughter's mind at ease.

When she got a little older, the daughter would ask her mother, why do the rabbis humiliate us by saying "to teach one's daughter Torah is to teach her foolishness"? And her mother would bring her all the answers and excuses in the world, and they didn't put her mind at ease.

When the daughter came of age, she would ask her mother, why do the men humiliate us, saying we're their property, and divorce is only at their will? And her loving mother would bring her all the answers and excuses in the world, and they didn't put her mind at ease.

When the days passed, and that girl became a mother, her little girl would pester her and ask her all the questions in the world, and she would bring her all the answers and excuses in the world, and they didn't put her mind at ease.

Psalm

ADAM SOL

We're late. She pulls on hose, as if her skin
were too sensitive for the air, and weaves

around the unmade bed, socks on the floor,
sweatpants failing to climb the desk chair.

She gathers papers, bumps me on my way
out of the bathroom, drops them, swears,

reshuffles, pecks my cheek to let me know
It's not you. 7:50. The service starts at eight.

I wait at the piano, play a tarantella.
The gray skirt suit broadens her shoulders,

very professional. Hair pulled back,
perfume subtle, earrings simple and elegant.

Most of the members only summer here: yachts
        on Lake Michigan.
In winter it's tough to get a minyan, but tonight,

there are not enough prayerbooks to go around.
        Maybe it's the new rabbi.
The rented church hums with voices,

and someone opens the front door
        to let some air into the place.
I sit next to Mel Feldman as he shoos his senile wife

from the gold earrings of the woman in front of us,
        dangling like wind chimes.
Oh Sylvie. He grips her hand in her lap, grits his teeth.

From the front come the welcoming remarks, then:
 Let us rise for the Bar'chu.
Mrs. Klein does her best with the ancient upright,

and the congregation lifts its wobbly voice
 for the summons prayer,
once sung with ram's horns. *Praised be the Lord,*

to whom our praise is due, now and forever.
 The first of many redundancies.
The young rabbi arranges the *kiddush* cup while we sing.

Praise for the Lighter of Fire, praise for the One
 Whose Word Makes
Evening Fall. The same pattern every time.

Praise for the God of our Fathers: Abraham, Isaac,
 and Jacob. The rabbi adds:
And for our mothers: Sarah, Rebecca, Rachel, and Leah.

The sermon is about bringing religion into our lives,
 and the rabbi performs it
with conviction, if not polish. She'd been revising it

until this afternoon. Final praise for the Source of Peace,
 for the One
Who Spread Out the Heavens and Established the Earth.

Whispers behind me: *That's the rabbi's husband.*
 Praise for Beverly Goldstick,
who is hosting the *Oneg*. Praise for everyone who helped her bake.

After the closing song, I am congratulated by blue blazers
 and lace wrists, gray smiles,
penciled eyebrows. *You must be so proud.* Praise

for the gossip of widows and divorcées.
     Praise for their pleasure,
for their uncritical awe, praise for what keeps

a tiny congregation together: history, stubbornness,
     dues from downstate.
Praise for the woman who has led them tonight,

drifting now among plastic cups of grape juice
     with her trademark tired smile.
Praise for these my hands, which will hold her hips and back,

Later, curtains drawn, when everyone is home and at rest.

Clearing Paths

Rabbi Deborah Waxman, PhD

THE RABBI of my childhood congregation gave me a warm hug every Shabbat; the rabbi of my teen years thrilled me with his intellectual challenges; and most every rabbi I met through United Synagogue Youth was welcoming. And they were all men. Even when I enrolled at Columbia University in 1985, a few blocks away from the Jewish Theological Seminary and just three years after the Conservative Movement began to ordain women, it still took several years before I met a rabbinical student or rabbi who was a woman. (Admittedly, I kept my distance from JTS, turned off by the rationale that a woman rabbi needed to become a halachic male and by the seminary synagogue that didn't yet count women in a minyan.) When I started to consider rabbinical school, it was clear that the Reconstructionist Rabbinical College, egalitarian since its earliest years, was the right seminary for me. I started twenty-five years after RRC's founding and only twenty years or so after the ordinations of Sally Priesand and Sandy Sasso. Women made up of half of RRC's student body by that point, and it took me several years to fully realize how recently that reality could have been possible. I am profoundly grateful to the women who bushwhacked a path for me and others to follow. Though at times my own journey has been full of weeds and stumps and other stumbling blocks, these pioneers cleared a way for my generation. In the Reconstructionist Movement, I have been able to grow powerfully as a human being, a rabbi, and a leader and to rise up to be the president and CEO of Reconstructing Judaism and RRC. That I am a woman and a lesbian is expressive of our shared commitments, and with the first generation of women rabbis' courage always in my mind, I strive to clear paths and make space for those who will follow after me.

Who Am I?

Rabbi Rebecca L. Dubowe

Who am I?
A woman rabbi
A Deaf rabbi
Woman or Deaf
Deaf or Woman
Who am I?

Who is God?
Is God Deaf?
Is God a woman?
Which one? Or both?

Does God have ears?
Do I have ears? My ears are broken and they are still on
    both sides of my head.
Does God have a voice? According to the Torah, at least 70
    of them.
Adonai, s'fatai tiftach, ufi yagid t'hilatecha.
Do I have a voice? My voice is loud and clear in my own
    unique way—from my lips to my hands.
Does God have hands?
Do I have hands? My hands are constantly signing,
    communicating, teaching, and creating a renewed
    sense of existence and validation for those who deserve
    to be embraced.

Is God a lover of life, a teacher of truth and acceptance? Yes.
What does it mean to be a rabbi? Who am I? A woman?
    Deaf?
No need to ask.

Just let me be who I am.

I am a Rabbi. I am a Woman. I am Deaf.

I am a lover of life, Judaism, people, truth, and acceptance for all of God's children.

Adonai, open up my lips, that my mouth [and hands] may declare Your praise.

No Voice of God

LEAH LAX

JUNE 3, 1972. I was sixteen and electrified, watching Sally Priesand on national news. A world was opening for women. I went to my rabbis, Irwin Goldenberg and Jack Bemporad, and both said: You can do this. You can do this!

Instead, Lubavitch came to town. I fell, hard, into a world drained of color where male rabbis with pious beards were its arbiters. For thirty years, I was both unable to conceive of a place among them as a lesbian and unable to pull away, until someone gave me a Hadassah Magazine, in it an interview of Rabbi Lisa Edwards. I got myself to Los Angeles. Lisa took me home, where I marveled at two women brushing their teeth together in the morning, then went into my room and wept. She gave me an essay by Rabbi Rachel Adler—in it, "I tear the words of Torah until they bleed like I do." New shock waves woke me up a little more.

The next morning, Rachel came and took me to her shul. When she draped her tallit over my shoulders, another boundary in my life melted away. The world became a nonbinary continuum of infinite possibility.

That afternoon, Rachel introduced me to Rabbi Sue Levi Elwell at her Shabbes meal.

Afterwards, I went home and resumed my role. Then I let myself fall in love. I let myself feel.

Months later, hours after a lawyer told me that, as a lesbian, I couldn't get custody of my children, Sue came to my city and called. "I faced the same," she told me over lunch, and "You can do this." So, I did. I did because three women rabbis who did not presume they spoke with the voice of God had passed me like a precious package one to the next and upheld my voice for me until I could hear.

What Comes Next

To Women Rabbis

JACQUELINE OSHEROW

In every Yiddish novel, there's invariably
an artisan—a needle-maker, a locksmith—
who pores over the Talmud in his back room
(he rarely has customers in his shop),
his study so disciplined, wide-ranging, deep
that scholars always bring their questions to him
and not to the overfed, brocaded rabbi
usually too busy acquiring wealth
to give the holy texts much attention.
Of course, I'm merely talking about fiction
written by *apikorsim* (the irreverent)
who traded *bais medrash* for coffee house,
but still: are we sure we want to do this?
Promise we'll be humble, worthy, different.

Women's Wisdom

RABBI SUE LEVI ELWELL, PHD

Women's wisdom builds this house.
— Proverbs 14:1

I ENTERED HUC-JIR in 1981 with what I thought were well-hewn tools of reading, investigation, and excavation. After years of researching Jewish women's stories, I immersed myself in a tradition where women's voices were rarely recorded. In one class, I remember feeling my whole body convulse as we confronted a classical text with a seemingly clinical discussion of the status of a woman who had been raped in war. Where was the holiness and the humanity in this exchange? A beloved male classmate attempted to calm me: "Sue! It's only a text!"

I knew then that I needed to acquire power tools to confront, reread, and interpret texts that were my inheritance. I found many of those tools beyond the walls of the classrooms and the extensive libraries of the college.

And so, as I completed my rabbinic studies, and throughout the decades of my rabbinate, I have studied and taught women's wisdom, asking questions and exploring ideas and possibilities that that were, then, beyond the curriculum. There are now many of us who have learned to wield new tools. Ever mindful of the essential humanity and vulnerability of each of our study partners, of each of our students, of each of our teachers, we are crafting bold, powerful, complex, and holy structures that mirror and expand our rich legacy of heated engagement. Like those before us, we too stumble. We get up, reassess and sharpen our tools, and reenter the sacred conversation. Women's wisdom builds this house.

78

A Wondrous Explosion

Rabbi Sharon Kleinbaum

I AM INSPIRED by the Holy Power of feminism.

The late *tzaddeket* bell hooks, *z"l*, wrote:

> Patriarchal masculinity teaches men that their sense of self
> and identity, their reason for being, resides in their capac-
> ity to dominate others.... Visionary feminism is a wise and
> loving politic.... Love can never take root in a relationship
> based on domination and coercion.

Baruch HaShem, feminism doesn't liberate only women. Men need
to be liberated. Fannie Lou Hamer, *z"l*, stated, "Nobody's free until
everybody's free."

As a feminist theologian, I see liberation extending further. Feminism doesn't liberate only human beings—it liberates Godself. It
shatters the constricting vessels of a God formed only in the mascu-
line. This revolution creates a wondrous explosion of divine possibilities for all.

Sally became a rabbi when I was fourteen. My entire childhood,
I never saw a woman rabbi. Clergy who transmit the word of God
reflect God to us. The absence of female rabbis profoundly constricted
my understanding of the power of prayer. The presence of women
rabbis over this half century has changed that.

I am blessed to be part of a *shalshelet*, a tradition of change in which
we ask God to be our partner. The struggle for racial justice, liberat-
ing Black and white. The feminist revolution, rescuing women, men,
and ultimately, all genders. LGBTQIA liberation, which in turn frees
straight people. These are all interconnected. They all expand our consciousness and enlarge our conception of God.

Liberation of humanity and God will never be done. *Lo alecha
ham'lachah ligmor* (Pirkei Avot 2:21) —we won't finish the job, but we
and God must keep working toward a wondrous explosion.

Finding My Voice

Rabbi Beth H. Klafter, RJE, DD

W HEN I CHOSE to become a rabbi nearly fifty years ago, I did so because I loved all things Jewish. I hungered for more knowledge and for the privilege of sharing it with others. I envisioned my role as a teacher and messenger of Judaism—something that happened outside of myself. I anticipated placing a gift package bursting with Jewish items and information into the hands of another Jew.

As I reflect on thirty-four years in the rabbinate, what surprises me is that being a rabbi often has much more to do with me than with the contents of that package. While I have learned more about Judaism and Jewish texts over the years, the rabbinate has taught me far more about myself. I have learned to find my own voice, to have the confidence and courage to believe that my ideas and perspectives matter. I have learned that my very presence can make a difference in profound ways, even when there are no words or texts to guide me. I have learned that I am strongest when I accept—and even disclose—my own vulnerability.

I have discovered that Judaism provides the language, but the message is mine.

Rightful Places

ERIKA DREIFUS

When, in our time, some still resist
  a woman's right to wear a prayer shawl,
    or read from the Torah,
      or study to be ordained as a rabbi,
who can be surprised that Judith's story
is excluded from the *Tanach*?

For if Judith—
  brave,
   articulate,
    smart,
     powerful,
      pious,
       latter-day
        Hanukkah heroine

had been granted admission to those holy pages,

how on earth, all these centuries later,
could anyone attempt to deny her daughters
their own rightful place?

To Have a Voice

RABBI SHAI HELD, PhD

GENESIS SAYS that God "fashioned the human being—dust from the soil—and breathed into its nostrils the breath of life, so that the human being became a living being [*nefesh chayah*]" (Genesis 2:7). Strikingly, the *Targumim* render "a living being" as a "speaking being" (*nefesh m'mal'la*). Implicit in their translation is a critical claim: to be fully alive as a human being is to speak, to have a voice, to be heard. There is an indignity that stems from forced silence, and a unique dignity that flows from speech.

To be part of the covenantal community, to live in relationship with the God of Israel, is to hear God's word and to discuss and interpret it. The Written Torah elicits the Oral Torah; we respond to God's speech with speech of our own.

In the first almost three thousand years since Sinai, women's voices were heard only from the margins and only as men reported hearing them. For the past fifty years, in contrast, women have spoken as never before; they have had a voice, and they are being heard. Though our communities still have a ways to go in hearing women's voices as equal in importance and urgency to men's, there is no overstating the importance of women's contributions to the conversations of Torah and Jewish life. Put simply, it is a triumph in the enduring struggle for human dignity for all; it is a victory for the very idea that we are all created in God's image, regardless of gender (Genesis 1:27).

To the pioneers who have led us into this new age of human dignity, thank you. We are in all your debt. May there be many more like you.

Rebekka the Voice Teacher

RABBI MÓNICA GOMERY

I'm standing in the bedroom of Rebekka
the voice teacher. Her hands harvest the keyboard.

She makes me look in the mirror,
barefoot while I breathe.

She lays me on the floor.
Puts a book on my stomach.

There is a diaphragm
somewhere inside me blooming

like a sea urchin.
Spines, a sharp tooth.

My breath plays catch and run.
My breath kicks the can.

My shoulders are doing
too much of the work.

She says, imagine a golf ball
in your mouth. Imagine an apple.

Lift your soft palate like a parachute.
Lift, lift, lift, she commands, but my tongue

might as well be my toes.
It stays on the ground.

My tongue yoked under the thumbs
of all the lost languages. She says, imagine

an orb of light in your mouth.
I drop a cupped hand into the well

of my throat. Gravel, glass,
and granola where there should be water.

Instead radio static, anxious baby birds,
one disoriented scorpion scratching.

She says, unspool the breath like a ribbon.
I am a horse tangled in ankles. I am a stairwell

on the wrong end
of a hammer.

Rebekka takes a breath, says
there's something I need you to know.

The horse in me stops braying.
My ankles quit hammering.

Your voice, she says, belongs
to centuries of mothers.

Mothers, and tantes
and babas and shvesters

and primas and spunkles and dodis
and saftas and bisabuelitas.

To people who were never
permitted to open their mouths.

No golf ball, no apple.
It belongs to a helix of shoulders

hunched into shoulders. To a voice
boxed into a voice, stuffed

with a popped lung. Your voice belongs to lost
transcripts, pruned fingers in dishwater, scraped

knees running from drunk soldiers in uniforms.
It is wool pulled over the questions

of women. A fist pulled over
their minds. And your body is buckled

by the weather of men.
I cry.

Rebekka cries. Her grandmother cries.
My grandmother cries.

And so they appear.
Processing across the black and white

keys, crossing the room like migrating birds.
Some moon-hipped. Some move how

an ant moves, thinking and purposeful.
Rachel and Leah and Chana and Ruth.

Naomi, Serach, Dina, and Orpa. Even Rachav.
Even Bat Paroh, renamed Daughter of Yah.

You might call them *the biblical women*, but
that's not what they are. They are thorns

birthing roses beside the hewn stones
of the Temple. They are hot grains

of sand, feet bruising continents
with all of that walk. Wide streets,

defiant rivers, they are cavern
of earth opening, empty with thirst.

They assemble on shelves, perch
the lips of the plant pots.

They circle and surround us, pull up
a chair. Steady in their line of sight, I

review what verbs I've inherited: run,
draw water, fill jars. Take a breath.

Rebekka the voice teacher pulls a red jacket
off the coatrack of my throat.

When I tell you to open your mouth more,
she says, it's so you can let out the ghosts.

No, not the ghosts.
Their clenched,

crabby shadows. She says,
imagine a wing in your mouth.

Estrogen-Enriched Judaism

Rabbi Marla J. Feldman

AFTER I WAS ORDAINED in 1985, I was the first and only woman rabbi in the communities I served in Sarasota, Orlando, and Gainesville, Florida. At times it was frustrating to be viewed as a woman rabbi rather than simply a rabbi, yet that burden also provided a platform and unique opportunities I may not have had otherwise.

Being the first led to many speaking opportunities during those years, and I often was asked if being a woman would shape my rabbinate. My response was that we all are shaped by various facets of our lives: where and how we were raised, our role models, our education, and of course, our gender. I see the world through women's eyes, just as I see the world through Jewish eyes. That refracted lens has helped shape and define my career.

Similarly, the presence of women in the rabbinate has helped shape Jewish life itself. Women rabbis have infused the community with their values and priorities, lifting up critical issues, creating new prayers and rituals, revisioning Jewish history, and providing new role models for the next generation. Our estrogen-enriched Jewish world is stronger and healthier for that infusion.

As a child, the rabbinate was not a career I could envision for myself. Now, when a young woman sees that possibility for herself, I know I have been part of a great evolution in Jewish life. It has been a blessing to bring my woman-rabbi perspective to my rabbinate and to those I have served over the years.

In Her Hands
Notes from a Soferet

RABBI BEC RICHMAN

I dunk my body in an inkwell of water
ready my hands, my heart, my lips
to speak words my ancestors
spoke, wrote, passed, told, `
buried.

At home, in the dark,
intention pours out like easy rain
and the quill—cut and ready—dips in
gathers close, holds tight.

Exhalation is whispering the words I will write
scratch of the quill on animal skin turned parchment
the low hum of the light—nothing more.

They forgot to tell us to keep our shoulders down
to keep our hair pinned back
to keep our bracelets off to the side
to make sure the babies were fast asleep before we wrote.

But I will not sign this work,
each scroll a mystery of inheritance.

Who wrote with a purple quill?
Who wrote with bellies full of babes, with breasts begging
   for release?
Who wrote hidden, who made their own ink, stretched
   their own hides?
Who passed on in hushed delivery?

In the studio, I rebel,
paint and write with what should not be ink
carve out letters, beg their emergence
impregnate Torah with my own birthing.

Back at the *mikveh*,
blue waters hold secrets
white space around black words, too:
processed skin, hair lines and splotches of color from a doe
echo our voices and our bodies
tuck us quietly into the telling.

A New Paradigm and a New Era

RABBI SHEILA PELTZ WEINBERG

WHEN I FIRST HEARD there were women who could become rabbis, I knew that I had to become a rabbi. I had no idea what it would mean for me or for Jewish history. Now I realize that these fifty years ushered in a new paradigm and a new era. Perhaps, it is the most significant event since the destruction of the Second Temple. We have barely begun to realize the radical nature and meaning of this shift. Three examples follow:

Women rabbis signaled the opening of multiple hierarchies that have been embedded in Jewish culture, learning, and spirituality. Rabbinic culture and leadership belonged exclusively to cisgender men. Now, not only women but lesbian, gay, bisexual, nonbinary, transgender, asexual, intersex, as well as Black and Brown Jews are moving into leadership positions. Jews have always inhabited the margins of society, but now the margins of Jewish society are moving into a more central place.

Women rabbis have reimagined spiritual leadership and creativity of embodied, earth-based spirituality. Women have classically been denigrated as being too earthy, disconnected from spirituality because of our own embodiment. Now, with the planet in danger and our alienation from nature revealed, groups like the Kohenet (Hebrew priestess) movement are opening pathways and rituals to reconnect us to our planet, celebrating our sacred partnership with the earth, recommitting to a sacred relationship of protection and care.

A final example is mindfulness in Judaism. Women rabbis brought Jews together to sit in silence. Silence and the cultivation of loving awareness can lead to the arising of profound connection as well as wisdom. Bringing people together in safe silence opens pathways to the sacred that have long been hidden.

In the Sanctuary of the Changing World

JAN FREEMAN

For Rabbi Caryn Broitman, and for Marcy Slater in memory

She appears on Friday evenings
Oseh shalom bimromav
hu yaaseh shalom aleinu
with my aunt's voice circling
(come and worship, this is new)
as the cardinal in spring, as the finch, the gull
We are connected, her lucky chosen, we are change
L'chah dodi likrat kalah p'nei Shabbat n'kab'lah
Without arrogance, without erasure
in conversation, in community
the window of her knowledge, safety and warning
our doorposts marked
Sh'ma Yisrael, Adonai Eloheinu, Adonai Echad
In the bodies of memories, in the shadows of grief
she welcomes, she davens, weaves the past into the present
Shameless her stance, her searching, her strength
as she inverts the childhood dictums, the mocking, the absence
Blessed are You, the Ancient One, our God, God of our ancestors
God of Sarah, God of Rebekah, God of Rachel, God of Leah
In the open air, imagination, the intellect, female
at the bimah by the sea
traditions leave, return expanded
This voice, the woman rabbi
from centuries of silence, our muted foremothers

Baruch atah Adonai, Eloheinu Melech haolam
asher natan lanu Torat emet
v'chayei olam nata b'tocheinu
She opens the doors of the sanctuary in the creation of sanctuary
My aunt's voice circles as it weaves
The rabbi rises, she questions, she unearths laughter
embodiment of comfort, embodiment of hope
Yitgadal v'yitkadash sh'mei raba
In the grace of her guidance, in the changing world of her wisdom
in celebration and in pain
we are alive in her sanctuary
and I say Amen.

Inside the Tent

Rabbi Denise L. Eger

FIFTY YEARS of women rabbis is but a drop in the timeline of Jewish history, and yet the impact of women rabbis upon Judaism is enormous. These rabbis, we rabbis, have shaped and reshaped Jewish life, scholarship, and community—every aspect of what it means to be Jewish and the very definition of Jewish communal life.

Women rabbis have brought a different set of questions to Judaism and different perspectives. These last fifty years of women rabbis has begun to chip away at the patriarchal overlay, allowing for a less hierarchical and more inclusive Jewish community. The ordination of women rabbis gave permission to others to imagine themselves inside our tent, when they had formerly been outside. This is directly related to the inclusion of the LGBTQ community and the efforts to include interfaith families.

It has been often slow going for women rabbis to achieve parity and equity with male colleagues. At times we have been shut out of the corridors of power and access in the organized Jewish community and overlooked in larger society. Women rabbis still don't receive the same salaries as many of our male colleagues. Women rabbis still face hurdles of misogyny. Women rabbis still face discrimination when it comes to being named as the senior rabbi of pulpits and as leaders of Jewish organizations. Women rabbis still face tremendous pushback from those in the Orthodox community who fail to recognize that the Jewish world has changed forever and that women rabbis' scholarship and leadership are here to stay.

I know I have been blessed to be able to engage the larger Jewish world with my efforts to welcome and include LGBTQ Jews into the mainstream of Jewish life. From the beginning of my rabbinate, I have tried to create safe space for learning about LGBTQ Jewish lives and for LGBTQ Jews to reconnect and explore Jewish communal life. I am proud that there is a blossoming of LGBTQ Jewish life that is no longer on the margins, but fully within the center of the Jewish people. The role of women in the rabbinate helped to make that dream a reality.

Why Do Women Rabbis Matter?

Rabbi Jacqueline Mates-Muchin

SOMEONE RECENTLY SHARED that they thought I might be from Mars. They meant it as a compliment. After reading a piece I wrote, they were struck that they had never before encountered a perspective like mine, and my teaching opened new possibilities for the way they look at Judaism.

My perspective is informed by being a middle-aged, Chinese female—different attributes from those of the person with whom I spoke and from the majority of those who have come before me in the rabbinate. Different life experiences offer new insights into our texts and tradition that can help expand people's understanding of what their lives could mean. Diversity in the rabbinate matters. Having women in rabbinic leadership positions these past fifty years has meant more teachings from a broader spectrum of the human experience, which makes Judaism relevant to more people and to the world in which we are living.

Women rabbis matter because our experiences and perspectives make life and Judaism whole.

A Pregnant Rabbi Officiates at the Wedding of an Ob-Gyn

KATHRYN HELLERSTEIN

It was hot that Vermont afternoon
In the pine grove
More than thirty years ago,
But what warmed my heart
Was the bride, my middle sister,
A doctor who delivered babies,
Escorted through the shade
By our parents toward the chuppah.
What made me sweat
Was my belly, heavy
Under pastel blossoms,
My ankles swelling,
And that baby-in-process
Turning somersaults inside me,
While under the chuppah
Stood the rabbi,
Even more pregnant than I.
She wrapped her tallis, as white as
The flower wreath on the bride's head,
Around her enormous dress
As it ballooned
In a momentary breeze,
Bringing a vision of
Expectancy and hope.

Not Sitting on the Sidelines

RABBI CAROLE B. BALIN, PhD

To BE HONEST, when I graduated high school in 1982—despite it being ten years since Sally's ordination—I thought about becoming a rabbi's wife. I had never seen a female rabbi and figured that by marrying a male rabbi, I could at least have a front-row seat to everything I loved about being a Jew: learning, teaching, praying, singing.

Voila! Four years at a women's college changed everything. I'd be damned if I was going to sit on the sidelines of Jewish life as a newly formed feminist. So six weeks after my Wellesley College commencement, I arrived in Jerusalem to start rabbinical school at HUC-JIR.

I didn't stop with the rabbinate. During my fourth year of rabbinical school, Professor Ellen Umansky, Wellesley '72, came to teach for a semester. In our Jewish feminist theology class, she assigned a manuscript version of the soon-to-be groundbreaking feminist classic *Standing Again at Sinai*, which she had just received from her friend, Judith Plaskow. Professor Umansky—with her manicured, red-polished nails and a miniskirt covering a pregnant belly—allowed me to see that I, too, could take the academic road to my professional future.

After being ordained and then earning a doctorate, I was appointed to the HUC-JIR faculty and felt like the proverbial "rose among the thorns." I was "Carole" among "Dr. Borowitz, Dr. Chernick, and Dr. Cohen." But lo and behold, a cohort of new female colleagues streamed in to bless me with their presence—and to raise up generations of students who would never doubt their God-given abilities, as I once had.

Birthrights

Rabbi Tamara R. Cohen

For Ayelet

Three sisters, two rabbis among them.
Perhaps they had to make up for the lost generations
The great-grandmother on one side who might have been the
    Baalat Shem Tov,
The great-great-grandmother on the other side whose
    compilations of legal rulings
were the only table she had ever set.

The second sister went first; just a decade after the doors were
    opened to women
(straight women, only, as was later clarified).
The second sister sat in cold classrooms taught by men whose
    eyes darted like almost invisible bugs
on the shimmery stillness of their Talmud tractates to their
    newly shapely students and then quickly back to the page.

Henrietta Szold had been granted permission to sit in those same
    rooms seventy years before.
Only to sit, not to seek status or access to a title kept from her by
    tradition and its self-appointed guardians; she would earn her
    place in history another way, Mother of Israel, like Deborah,
    with no progeny save the orphans of *Judenrein* Eastern Europe.

The elder sister, six blocks downtown from where the second
    sister lay *t'fillin* in the mornings,
lay awake in the arms of her closeted lover, weary yet restless
    from failed attempts to testify to her fitness to serve the Jewish
    people, good lesbian daughter deserving of her own open door.

The second sister purchased two copies of the Rabbi's Manual
with its gold lettering and multiple black ribbon bookmarks
designed to hold the places of commonly used ceremonies—
funeral, wedding, birth of a daughter. She gave one to the
elder sister, who took it and began to do what rabbis do.

Twenty years later she too found herself with an additional
name, two rounded over Hebrew letters like sisters studying
beside each other, mourning, celebrating, teaching each other
the secrets of the world, and how to change it.

Rav: a teacher.

Another interpretation: Enough. As it says: Enough of sitting in
the valley of tears.

Another interpretation: Multiple. As it has come to be once
again, a mixed multitude crossing into freedom through walls
of water, with feet on dry land.

A Reflection from Thirty-Three Years in the Rabbinate

RABBI AMY SCHWARTZMAN

I AM GRATEFUL for a long and fulfilling career in the rabbinate in a dynamic congregation that has proudly embraced a diverse group of clergy over many years. In 1990 I became Temple Rodef Shalom's first assistant rabbi and only eight years later its second senior rabbi.

For all of my thirty-three years in my congregation, I have felt accepted, appreciated, and supported, and yet once in a while I am reminded that female-identified rabbis, despite our growing numbers, are not fully embraced even in the most progressive of communities.

A few years ago, during our monthly family Shabbat, I was telling a Chelm-like story about a troubled soul who sought out the advice of a local rabbi. As I described the scene, I identified the rabbi as "she." A wave of laughter spread through the congregation, and my heart sank. I had served this temple for decades, and yet hearing the rabbi identified as female brought on snickers and chuckles.

I love my congregation; it is an exceptionally warm and caring community. I have no doubt that my impact has been positive and far-reaching. And yet . . . and yet . . . and yet.

Joys Along the Way

Rabbi Juliana Schnur Karol

FIFTY YEARS AGO, the creative potential of the Jewish people was unleashed. The great joy of ordaining women has its locus in the boundless possibility for expanding the definition of who rabbis are, what Torah they bring to the world, and how they expand belonging by their sheer existence. Rabbi Sally Priesand didn't just mark the beginning of women's ordination; she opened the door to all genders, all abilities, and to the still-to-be-realized hope for a truly inclusive rabbinate. My joy as a woman rabbi exists in the invitation each day to newly define what "rabbi" means for my congregants. I am a rabbi who dances. I am a rabbi who mothers. I am a rabbi who lifts up the voices of other women and nonbinary thinkers. I am a rabbi who stumbles and learns and shares and grows. And I pray that in my woman body and with my woman soul, I bring joy, comfort, and sacred witness to the community and the people who call me rabbi.

All In

RABBI JOUI M. HESSEL, RJE

I LOVED The Brady Bunch as a young child. I wanted to be like Marcia (of course) and enjoyed watching Greg, Peter, Bobby, Marcia, Jan, and Cindy get into and out of funny situations. In retrospect, I now see how the show utilized typical gender roles: boys played doctor, girls played nurse; boys grew into "men," while the girls remained "girls."

At the time, I imagined that I would grow up to be a performer or a real estate developer (the family business). Even though I loved my Jewish day school in Miami and soon began to fall in love with URJ Camp Coleman, becoming a Jewish professional was not on my radar.

I had met only a few female rabbis by the time my synagogue sent me to HUC-JIR for the IRSTA Program (Institute for Religious School Teaching Assistants). Synagogues and summer camps were most likely to have male rabbis, so I never considered becoming a rabbi. Indeed, I loved so much about Judaism (learning, debating, writing, rituals, and social justice, to name a few) that as soon as I was told that I could become a rabbi too, I was all in!

Today, after having served for thirteen years in a large congregation and for four years in organizational roles, I treasure the moments when children ask me if "boys can become rabbis too." While the glass ceiling may have been shattered by Rabbi Sally J. Priesand, the shards of glass are still ever-present and can be sharp. One day, female rabbis will be called simply "rabbi." One day, congregants will not immediately refer to us as "Rabbi First Name" while our male counterparts are "Rabbi Last Name." And one day, children will look at each other and simply wonder who among them will become a rabbi when they grow up.

Rabbi's Daughter

NOMI STONE, PhD

From afar, the feeling sails toward
Me in white-hilled waves

As my dad, robed, on tiptoes,
Lifts his heels,

Springing up each time higher,
Holy Holy Holy;

When I was a child I wanted to become
A rabbi too, tracing

The Temple's map
To wonder, its rites and acts,

But I became a poet, lifting then falling into
The earth's wet flowers, struggling

To be good, to find clothes for this
Bright feeling,

Carrying language in bundles:
Hello little gods in the leaves,

In the eaves, let us double
Your world with our words.

The Presence of Women Rabbis

RABBI DAVID SAPERSTEIN

THE PRESENCE of women rabbis, in Reform Jewish life particularly and in so much of the Jewish community more broadly, has had enormous impact on my life, my career, and my work at the Religious Action Center (RAC). Of those ordained in the first decade or so after Sally J. Priesand, so many were champions of social justice who became key allies in our work. They were among our earliest Eisendrath legislative assistants (LAs) who went on to become distinguished Reform, Reconstructionist, and Conservative rabbis. Together with laywomen who were strong leaders of the Commission on Social Action, that first generation of women rabbis helped focus the RAC's legislative efforts on women's rights issues, even as some testified for us on such issues before Congress. I will single out Rabbi Laura Geller as representing many who profoundly influenced my thinking and shaped my views on public policy issues.

Rabbi Lynne Landsberg became my first major hire. She served for years as the RAC's associate director, a constant guide for us on issues of inclusion. The influence on our work when, for example, three early LAs, including two rabbis, were simultaneously serving as president of the CCAR (Rabbi Janet Marder), director of the Commission on Social Action (Rabbi Marla Feldman), and lay chair of the CSA (Jane Wishner) was palpable. So too when the RAC hired Rabbi Sharon Kleinbaum as director of congregational relations, who was one of, if not the very first, openly gay rabbi hired to serve a synagogue or denominational entity. I was blessed to learn from each of them, and so many others, and remain inspired by their legacies.

Park Slope / Chelsea

JASON SCHNEIDERMAN

The first time my mother saw a female rabbi,
flanked by a woman cantor, a woman gabbai,
and a rather butch mohel, she said, "They don't
want to be equal, they want to be *men*."

The way she said it surprised me. The way
men might be a shameful thing to be, the way
it entailed betrayal, of my mother, who wanted
no men on her side of the *m'chitzah*.

In those years, my only relationship to God
was anger. My only relationship to Judaism
was my own sense of betrayal that there was
no room for me if I were to love men. I can

understand wanting to be a man. It's great.
I love being a man. I love being with men. It
was a journey, but I got here. When my own
rabbi spoke about Abraham as a father

who hears voices telling him to harm his son,
I nearly burst into tears. She said, "If you feel
like you don't belong, you are having the most
Jewish feeling in the world, and you belong."

I kept going back to the synagogue where
my rabbi said the things I was thinking, where
my rabbi shaped my thinking week after week,
until I felt like I belonged and I felt like I could

see myself as the kind of Jew that made sense
to me. My mother was a teacher. Like me,
she had patience for students, but no one else.
If she were here, I'd remind her that rabbi

just means teacher. She was a rabbi all along.

From Strength to Strength

Rabbi Jacob Blumenthal

IN CONVERSATION with women who serve as rabbis and in other leadership positions in the Conservative/Masorti Movement, I often ask, "How did you end up in this role?" And the most common answer is "Until I was a teenager I didn't have a role model. And then a woman rabbi came into my community, and I could see myself as a leader."

Since the Jewish Theological Seminary ordained Rabbi Amy Eilberg as the first female Conservative rabbi in 1985, women have played key roles in the Conservative/Masorti rabbinate and our movement. Today, women compose more than 20 percent of the membership of the Rabbinical Assembly, with that percentage growing each year. Women rabbis have served, and continue to serve, in key roles in our movement: as president and CEO of the RA, as cochair of the Committee on Jewish Law and Standards and authors of some of its most important and groundbreaking *t'shuvot*, and as leaders in communal settings and in pulpits throughout North America, Latin America, Europe, and Israel.

Our women colleagues bring a unique lens to our traditions and texts, refashioning patriarchal traditions and structures and making our movement ever more relevant, just, and meaningful. Our diversity has become the strength of Conservative Judaism, and of the Conservative rabbinate in particular. May our women colleague rabbis continue to lead us *michayil l'chayil*—from strength to strength.

It Had Never Occurred to Me

RABBI SHELLEY KOVAR BECKER

TRUTHFULLY, the ordination of Sally was no more than "something to see" when I first heard of it. It did engender in me a curiosity to attend a service she was leading.

Then, in the early 1980s, I wanted a career change. I was in retail, where Friday eves and Saturdays were important times to be "in the office," and I was increasingly unhappy with the difficulty I was experiencing between my work and Jewish observance. I decided to explore a "Jewish" career, which would, possibly, give me the opportunity to link the professional and spiritual.

I was active in temple lay leadership, and one of my tasks was to hire religious school teachers. Living close to HUC-JIR in New York City, I had the opportunity to interact with student rabbis, cantors, and educators and to attend programming at the seminary. I was excited by the environment and study.

I decided to speak to the rabbi of my synagogue about my growing interest. We discussed teaching and other career paths when he said, "You know, women are now rabbis." It had never occurred to me to become one, though the idea of marrying a rabbi had. I had been an active child and teen participant in my home congregation (Riverdale Temple, Bronx, NY) and had met (all male) student rabbis over the years. This started a process of thought and especially discussion with my husband of ten years (not a rabbi), who would be most impacted if I were to pursue this incredible ideal. I began in Jerusalem in 1986 and was ordained at the age of forty-two.

In my student experience, my husband was briefly mistaken for the rabbi at my first holiday pulpit—he had the beard—and one male congregant there announced he would not attend my "female led" service. At another synagogue, my senior was a woman, and so it was natural for them to welcome me and my husband in our roles.

The "oys" were many, but the "joys" are incalculable. I would not have, could not have done this, but for the *vatikot* who preceded me.

An Older Woman

Rabbi Suzanne Singer

WHEN, AT THE AGE OF FORTY-TWO, I went back to school to become a rabbi, it never occurred to me that I could not do so because I am a woman. After all, this was twenty-five years after Sally Priesand had been ordained. I had spent twenty years as an Emmy Award–winning television producer, but unclear about my true path. When I finally received the call, it took me another ten years to believe in myself and to explore questions such as: Could I start all over again? But my gender was never an issue in my deliberations.

I am so grateful that I was afforded the opportunity to change the course of my life, and I feel so privileged to be a rabbi. The biggest stumbling block in my career has not so much been my gender per se, but the fact that I am an *older* woman. Synagogues seem to be looking for young rabbis, hoping to attract millennials, Gen Z-ers, and young families with children. I think it's time for the Reform Movement to reassess this premise. After all, one of the biggest youth heroes in recent history was the octogenarian Bernie Sanders! Aren't wisdom and experience vital assets in a rabbi, even in an older *woman* rabbi? Isn't it high time we stop thinking of older women as crones ready for the ash heap?

Chuppah, Chelsea, May 2000

STEPHANIE BURT

The world is a terror and has no place for me.
Wait. Stop. Rewind.

    And here comes Rachel the Rabbi,
Who asks us leading questions about Stevie Wonder,
Whose job is literally to believe in things,
In things that are not things, who knows love is not
One thing, or just a thing, or just one of those things
And knows that weddings are not wedding rings
Or prophecies or property exchange —

Smash glass, hold hands, do cry, don't set out
To do crimes (as in "be gay, do crimes") but if
You're illegal, she can help. She knows how to set up
That billowy, long-revered top
And the canopy underneath, and what to say.
(From one angle it's an *alef*. From
Another, a *mem*, or a *hei*.)

And if the public performance of affection
Between a girl and a girl or a boy and a boy
And a boy who is really a girl is a kind of rope trick,
A walk on a wire in any direction, then
The liturgy that wants us is a net
To catch us after confidence theatrics,
Its lines and grids the one that hold in place
A bedspring supporting a mattress for cuddling,
And linens, crisp for rest before next day.

A Reawakened Dream

Rabbi Lisa D. Grant, PhD

I WAS IN HIGH SCHOOL when Sally J. Priesand was ordained. Honestly, it didn't make much of an impression on me. If anything, I noted it as another hopeful sign of more career possibilities opening up to women, but becoming a rabbi was far from my heart and mind at that time.

Twenty years later, I was in Israel and heard a radio program interviewing Naamah Kelman, the first woman ordained in Israel. Now that was significant! As the interview progressed, it was clear that this was the same Naamah Kelman I had known at Camp Ramah in 1970. Also, by the early '90s, I was starting to make a dramatic career shift into the world of Jewish scholarship, along with deepening my Jewish life. Hearing that Naamah became a rabbi in her thirties planted a seed of possibility in me. Even as I was pursuing doctoral studies, I thought that maybe I too could become a rabbi.

Naamah and I met again in the late 1990s, when I was working on my dissertation. Soon after that, I was hired onto the faculty at HUC-JIR in New York, which gave me the gift of her continuing colleagueship and friendship. Eventually, after I had attained tenure and become a full professor, another rabbi colleague and friend, Rabbi Andrea Weiss, encouraged me to reawaken my dream of becoming a rabbi, which I achieved, studying alongside my students, in 2017.

To be sure, Sally's ordination remains a major milestone for all of us, but for me personally, it was these two firsts—Rabbi Naamah Kelman as the first female rabbi to be ordained in Israel and Rabbi Andrea Weiss as the first female provost and senior rabbi of HUC-JIR—who were my personal inspirations for becoming a rabbi. I am forever grateful for their encouragement, support, and friendship.

Worlds within Worlds

Rabbi Rachel Timoner

Just as we celebrate how far women have come in the rabbinate, we're reminded that the struggle for women's and gender equality is far from over.

Would anyone have believed for the last fifty years that in 2022 rabbis would be raising money for abortion funds and organizing underground networks to get women illegal but necessary health care because our bodies have been once again commandeered as reproductive vessels by the state?

Lest we feel that no progress has been made in the bleak landscape of Christian authoritarian triumph, we look around and find women in roles of leadership and authority throughout the Reform Movement. We hear the voices of women rabbis inveighing against the patriarchal backslide of our time. We see young women watching their seasoned elders, who have been leading for half a century, offering certainty that people of all genders have a place to lead here. And we find that we have created—are creating—worlds within our world: counterexamples of what feminist society can look like, of what egalitarian, pluralistic, and wonder-based religious life can be. These lived models nourish a parched landscape, just like Miriam's networks of wells slaked the thirst of a nation after the Israelites believed they had marched to freedom only to find themselves in a new and foreboding wilderness. Let us drink deeply from those wells as we make it through this wilderness and match the courage of our foremothers as we continue to lead on.

An Offering Made in Honor of Those Who Have No Time to Make an Offering

RABBI KAREN BENDER

For the women
the rabbis
who haven't the time
to contribute to this
tapestry
because just
as they sit down
to write
the phone rings
and just as they
wake up with an idea
the baby cries
and just as they
finally find the hour,
the kid needs
help with the homework,
and just as they
squeeze the ten minutes
into a Shabbat afternoon
to make this offering,
exhaustion sets in
and they fall asleep.

For the women
The heroic rabbis
The friends

And role models
Who haven't the time
To contribute to this
Tapestry

I, we
say thank you
we say you are
not forgotten
this time.

An Even More Expansive Future

RABBI ELLIOT KUKLA

Iᴛ'ꜱ ᴍᴀʏ 14, 2006, at the Wilshire Boulevard Temple, Los Angeles. I am at my ordination dressed in a new navy suit and a purple tie. It's the first time I have worn a man's suit in public. I also have a new name and pronoun that I have been trying on for size for the past few months. All these new things feel stiff and awkward on my body. Like my newly tailored suit, I am still "breaking in" my new gender identity. Bringing this part of myself, which I nurtured silently and secretly for so many years, to the surface is scary, painful, and spiritually exhilarating.

I am the first openly transgender rabbi to be ordained by HUC-JIR or by any rabbinical seminary. I am also the first nonbinary rabbi. As I step up to the bimah to become a rabbi, I am held and anchored by so many who came before me, who changed the definition of what it means to be a rabbi and created space for more embodiments of the Divine. I take a deep breath as Rabbi Ellenson lays his hands on my head, and I enter into this other golden chain of tradition, which stretches from Tamar to Beruriah to Sally Priesand, to the first gay and lesbian rabbis. I am here because they came before me. And I am dreaming of an even more expansive future.

When the Rabbi Asks for the Envelope

JULIE R. ENSZER

to mail the authorized application
to the Marriage Bureau,
after she has supervised
our signatures and signing
by witnesses, I say,
Oh, I *can mail it.*
No, *that's my job*, she intones
gleefully. And for a moment
I withhold the mail carrier, meekly
adding, But I *have a stamp.*
She laughs. I release the envelope
with reticence. That moment,
I lost all control; the beloved and I
no longer strangers under the law.

The Rabbinate Was Never Closed to Me

RABBI ASHIRA KONIGSBURG

I WAS LUCKY ENOUGH to grow up in a time when the path to the rabbinate was never closed to me. I benefited from all the struggling, suffering, persisting—and glass ceiling breaking—of those women who preceded me in the rabbinate. Because of them, I could casually find my rabbinic journey. Because others were first, I didn't think of myself as a groundbreaker. Because others were first, I was free to find my own path at my own pace.

I was also free to think of myself not as a "woman rabbi," but just as a rabbi who was also female-identified, which is why it still comes to me as a surprise when gender dynamics show up in the way people relate to my leadership. Fortunately, I can then turn to the original pioneer women in the field, who are so generous in sharing their hard-earned wisdom with those of us in the next generations. From them I have learned how to stand up for myself and for my ideas, to be uncompromising when facing bias, and most importantly, to not believe in barriers, especially if they haven't (yet) been broken.

Compelled by the "Almosts"

RABBI JILL MADERER

ALTHOUGH I HAVE HEARD MANY say the overturning *Roe v. Wade* is a result of the defeat of Hillary Clinton's presidential candidacy, I would put it differently. The overturning of *Roe v. Wade* and the defeat of Hillary Clinton are the result of the same reality: the misogyny at the heart of society's refusal to accept women's agency.

I believe this rejection of women's full agency explains the inequality that remains in many women's leadership experiences and in the systems that continue to oppress women and gender nonconforming people, who through their leadership or their gender expressions challenge restrictive gender roles. The rabbinate is not immune.

And yet, I have hope. One source of my hope lies in the stories of those women who before 1972 almost became rabbis. The historical "almosts" inspire me with the steps they took and remind me to look for the almosts today—those people in our midst who are taking steps that may bring us to our next moment of progress.

The stories of the almosts compel us to ask: What should the Jewish community have understood and acted upon one hundred years ago, and today what should *we* understand and act upon now, for the sake of community, equity, and the future of the Jewish people? Right now, who is showing us the future?

Rabbi Sally J. Priesand opened doors. In pursuit of gender justice and beyond, for whom do we need to hold the door open?

A Rabbi Who Was Once a Girl

Rabbi Emily Langowitz

IN MY FIFTH YEAR of rabbinical school, I taught eighth grade at the congregation where I was an intern. I spent my time teaching a bunch of teens topics I thought they would enjoy: "Emotional Judaism," "Mussar Yoga," "Judaism and Gossip." I wanted, so desperately, to relate to them, the way I had felt related to by my female clergy and educators. One night, over the pizza dinner we were served before class began, I sat with the girls who were worrying about their outfits and their hair and fitting in, in the way that preteens do. I, wanting to fit in as much as they did, told them how I used to wear my hair, how silly I looked, and that it all turned out fine, only to look up and meet the eyes of a bright, fantastic kid with the exact same haircut.

Of all the things I learned in rabbinical school, the teachings of that moment may have been most important for who I am as a rabbi, but especially for who I am as a rabbi who was once a girl. I learned that my power is not in joining their insecurities to my own, but in lifting them up by showing them their own sparkling magnificence. It's carried me through ramen noodles at confirmation retreats, discussions with girls, teens, and grandmothers, and so much more. What is my job as a female rabbi? To reflect back to others how absolutely wonderful they are; to model that I believe that about myself, too, despite my mistakes and imperfections.

Love As Strong As Death

Nessa Rapoport

For Rabbi Naamah Kelman, first woman to become a rabbi in Israel

Unquenched after all these years, a thirst for love that
is not consumed, incarnate and transcendent, carnal
and immaculate, innocent. Can I embody you, be a
dwelling place for a spirit that partakes of all that lasts,
encompassing mistakes, and appetites, and prodigal
generosity, and terror and absolution, and whatever is
most frightening about becoming human. You, carrying
your pail ahead of me, spilling mercy and forgiveness
daily, calling my name at the same moment I am
conjuring you, a voice of unpolluted clarity, half a
world away, beside, within me. You, my theological
relief, my proof that even in the midst of unslaked
cruelty at the end of a barbaric century, nothing less
than a divinity could have tendered what you give me,
and allowed that in my being on earth I give to you.

Belonging as a "Woman Rabbi"

RABBI NIKKI DEBLOSI, PHD

SIMPLY DECLARING that I am "a rabbi, not a 'woman rabbi'" does nothing to change the underlying structures and assumptions that continue to hold back our progress as a Reform Movement.

I want to be accepted and celebrated as a woman and a rabbi because I want to eradicate the notion that there is an ideal rabbi, a standard model—white, heterosexual, male, Ashkenazic, etc.—against whom all others are labeled lesser than, deficient, exceptional, strange. Erasing the specificity of my gender or any other aspect of my identity that does not fit a narrow stereotype of "rabbi" might open doors professionally. But at what cost? How much of myself must I leave at the threshold?

As Jews, we should know deeply that difference and distinction and variety are not the problem.

When we bless "separation" at Havdalah, we don't say, "Thank God there's Shabbat, so we only have to tolerate those horrible six days temporarily." No! We say instead, "Thank God there are different kinds of time."

I want to say: Thank God there are different expressions of sex and gender. Thank God for women rabbis, and nonbinary bet mitzvah students, and transgender cantors, and interfaith families, and folks who have chosen Judaism in myriad ways. None "lesser than." None the "default." None the "exception." None the "distraction." All feeling truly as though we belong.

Can Boys Be Rabbis Too?

Rabbi Ashley Berns-Chafetz

"Mommy, can boys be rabbis too?"

I looked over at my six-year-old daughter, Zoe, in disbelief at her simple six-word sentence. Raised in a community with both male- and female-identifying rabbis, she knew the answer to her own question. Yet, as she sat by my side watching the Women Rabbinic Network's "Jubilee Inaugural: WRN Celebrates 50 years of Women in the Rabbinate," it was as if she were overtaken by the power and pride of the hundreds of female-identifying rabbis in the Zoom room. She listened intently as each speaker shared words of their journey in the rabbinate, the impact of Rabbi Sally J. Priesand's monumental ordination, and the work that continues today to continue breaking the glass ceiling.

I am proud that Zoe and my younger daughter, Mia, are being raised in a community that celebrates the accomplishments of rabbis, regardless of their gender. And even more so, I hope that as the daughters of a woman rabbi, they see that they do not have to choose between a career or parenthood, between work or home life. The opportunities are endless for them because we stand on the shoulders of others who worked tirelessly for the title of rabbi, to sit at the head of the table, and to stand on the bimah leading communities across the world. And maybe, just maybe, one day they will join this beautiful group and decide they too want the title of rabbi and to proudly lead the Jewish community.

A Metaphor of Holiness No Longer!

Rabbi Jan Katz

DA LIFNEI MI ATAH OMEID—"Know before whom you stand!" This is the phrase emblazoned over the ark in many a synagogue, reminding us that we should be filled with respectful awe in the presence of God. Although not a feature of the exquisite holy ark in Temple Emanu-El, the site of rabbinic ordination for graduates of HUC-JIR in New York, these words were palpable and real for me at the moment of my ordination on May 2, 2021 / 20 Iyar 5781, at the age of seventy-three years. Standing at right angles to the ark, with God's presence at my side, I faced provost Rabbi Andrea Weiss. In that moment, images flashed of all the gender barriers, innuendos, and challenges that Rabbi Weiss assuredly overcame to enable me to soar through rabbinical school in a perceived reality of equal access and respect. In that moment, I was simultaneously proud and humbled to live the dream of ordination by another woman and cherished teacher. Reflected in Rabbi Weiss's face were the brave women who paid forward to me their own scholarship, voices, and resilience during my four-year tenure at HUC-JIR, among them Rabbi Wendy Zierler, PhD, Dr. Sharon Koren, Rabbi Tamara Cohn Eskenazi, PhD, and my home rabbi and mentor, Rabbi Debbi Till.

In that moment, I was open, receptive, and alert—feeling loved, called, and connected. I was in God's presence.

The Only Ones

RABBI ARIEL TOVLEV

"YOU MIGHT BE THE ONLY ONE," I was told. For so long, people like me weren't allowed to become rabbis or cantors. For centuries only cisgender heterosexual men were Jewish clergy.

Brave women willing to be the only ones helped change our culture to see leaders in more of our members. Like Miriam at the parted shores, these women crossed a great divide toward liberation, inviting others to follow.

When I entered rabbinical school, there had only been two out trans students before me. At times I felt so isolated. It helped to speak with women who knew how it felt to be the only one in a room. This simple solidarity solidified my conviction that we are at the forefront of a new cultural shift.

Since starting rabbinical school, there has not been a single new cohort of students without at least one trans or nonbinary person. Although I had prepared myself to be alone, I am not alone. With every student who pushes boundaries, we pave the path for future leaders to be their full authentic selves.

We gather again at the great divide, dancing toward freedom. At first we felt alone, but hand in hand, we cross together: each of us a thin thread in the tapestry of the Jewish people.

Trans clergy may feel new, but our world is changing, and we are the agents of change.

I thought I would be the only one. But now I am one of many.

What Comes Next

JUDITH ROSENBAUM, PhD

"*IF YOU CAN SEE IT, you can be it.*" This precept—core to my work at the Jewish Women's Archive—speaks to the necessity of role models and the impact of representation. To be sure, the presence of women as rabbis on the bimah, in the classroom, at the sickbed, communal table, and boardroom, has transformed the assumptions and expectations of women and girls about their own capacities and opportunities, opening the door to generations of new leaders.

The fight for access can sometimes be mistaken for the goal itself, but it is, of course, only the first step. What comes next is far more important: the new vision, imagination, wisdom, and creativity that those who have historically been excluded or silenced bring to the tradition, fundamentally expanding and renewing it. Herein lies the beauty (and the terror) of change: it unfolds in ways we cannot always foretell, and it sparks revolutions. The presence of women in the rabbinate, for example, has highlighted the need for greater inclusion along other lines, such as race, sexuality, and disability, and has revealed ongoing inequality and discrimination in Jewish institutions.

In the scope of history, fifty years is not a long time. And in just these fifty years, what was once unimaginable has become foundational. As a historian, I am awed by the creativity sparked by women in the rabbinate, and I anticipate with excitement the continued pursuit of equity and the revitalization of Jewish life, community, and authority. This is only the beginning.

Here I Am

DORIS TRAUB

a daughter
committed to the commandments
called to chant the words of the prophets
but no *yad* will yield to my hand, no miniature metallic
finger will I point to precious parchment. Girls do not yet
   read from
Torah in my shul—a modest distance maintained in this
   sacred assembly.

Here you are,
years later, beckoning to my
daughter with an invitation to chant the
parsha on Rosh HaShanah, an offer that opens
out to summon her sisters until it finally fully unfolds:
     Would you like to join your daughters in reading Torah?

Drawing the females
of this family close into a sacred
semicircle on the bimah, tented under your tallit,
you place a silver filigree pointer into a feminine hand.
Passed from palm to palm to palm until words of the divine
finally fill a humble hungry mouth. My voice trembles:
   Hineini.

Glossary

Aliyah: Hebrew word meaning "ascent"; can mean both immigrating to Israel and reciting the blessings for the Torah reading.

Amcha: Hebrew word meaning "Your people," often used to simply mean "people."

Baruch HaShem: Hebrew phrase meaning "blessed is God," often used to offer informal thanks (e.g. in response to the question, "how are you?" one might respond, "*baruch hashem*").

Beit Din: Hebrew term meaning "house of law"; usually refers to a rabbinic adjudication panel.

Beit Midrash: Hebrew term meaning "house of study."

Bensch: Yiddish word meaning "to recite the blessings after a meal"; in this case, to lead such blessings publicly, an honor not permitted to women before this era.

Bet Mitzvah: A gender-inclusive term for the Jewish coming of age ceremony for people who identify as gender-fluid or nonbinary; can also be used as a plural term to replace the gendered *b'nei/b'not mitzvah* (sons/daughters of the commandments).

B'nei Mitzvah: Hebrew term meaning "sons/children of the commandments"; in colloquial American English, a coming-of-age ceremony celebrated by reading from and reciting the blessings over the Torah for the first time, usually around the age of thirteen.

B'not Mitzvah: Hebrew term meaning "daughters of the commandments."

B'rit: Hebrew word meaning "covenant"; can refer to the covenant between God and Israel or between people. It is also used as a shorthand way to refer to *b'rit milah* (i.e., bris), the covenantal ceremony of circumcision.

B'tzelem Elohim: Hebrew term meaning "in the image of God" from Genesis 1:27, reflecting the idea that all humanity is created equally and that everyone deserves equal respect and dignity.

Chesed: Hebrew word meaning "love, benevolence, kindness, grace." This is the fourth of the ten *s'firot* (mystical emanations of God).

Chuppah: The wedding canopy, representing the home a new couple will build together.

Dayeinu: Hebrew word meaning "it is enough for us," or "it would have been enough for us"; part of the refrain of a popular Passover reading and song.

G'vurah: Hebrew word meaning "strength"; the fifth of the ten *s'firot* (mystical emanations of God).

Gabbai: Aramaic word for "collector," originally indicating a tax collector; now used to refer to the person who facilitates and assists with the reading of the Torah.

Havdalah: Ritual conducted on Saturday night that formally separates Shabbat and the remainder of the week, with a focus on the division of holy and mundane, light and dark.

Hineini: Hebrew word meaning "here I am"; often the response of prophets and other biblical figures to God's call. It signifies that the speaker is in a place of spiritual readiness and receptiveness.

Judenrein: German term meaning "free of Jews" that was used by the Nazis to describe their goal for Europe.

Kavanah: Hebrew word meaning "intention" or "direction"; colloquially used to refer to the desire to set one's intention in a fitting spiritual and emotional place in order to be fully present for the sanctity of prayer.

K'hilah K'doshah: Hebrew term meaning "holy community."

Kippah: Traditional head covering won by Jews.

Kohenet: Hebrew word meaning "priestess"; also the name of an organization and a title for individuals working toward embodied, feminine, earth-based Jewish practice.

L'dor Vador: A Hebrew term meaning "from generation to generation."

Leyn: Yiddish word meaning to chant from a Torah scroll, an honor not permitted to women before the present era.

Lokshen kugel: Yiddish term referring to a traditional Ashkenazic baked sweet dish made with noodles.

Maftir: Hebrew word meaning "one who concludes"; used to refer to the last person called to the bimah for the honor of the Torah blessings (aliyah laTorah) on Shabbat and holiday mornings. This person sometimes also reads the haftarah from the books of the Prophets.

Mechitzah: A divider used in Orthodox Jewish sanctuaries to separate men from women; often seen as a symbol of the oppression of women and non-binary people in Orthodox religious spaces.

Parsha: Aramaic term for "portion"; often used to refer to parshat hashavua, the Torah portion of the week.

Shechinah: Hebrew word meaning "dwelling" (sometimes translated as "She who dwells within"); refers to the female name and aspect of God. In Jewish mysticism, Shechinah (also called Malchut) is the lowest of the ten s'firot (mystical emanations of God) and therefore the aspect of God that is closest to humanity.

Sh'leimut: Hebrew word meaning "wholeness"; it shares a root with the word shalom.

S'michah: Hebrew word meaning "laying on [of hands]"; refers to rabbinic ordination.

Soferet: A female scribe of the Torah.

T'filah: Hebrew word meaning "prayer."

T'fillin: Commonly translated as "phylacteries"; two black leather boxes containing parchment scrolls with words of Torah that are worn during weekday morning prayer on the arm and head of the person praying.

T'shuvot: Jewish legal responsa given in answer to sh'elot, Jewish legal questions.

Taamod: Hebrew word meaning "stand up" (feminine singular); used to call a woman up to the bimah for the honor of the Torah blessings (aliyah laTorah). For most of Jewish history, women were not permitted to be called to the Torah; the power of hearing this feminine form cannot be overestimated.

Tanach: The Hebrew bible. This word is an acronym of the Hebrew words for Torah, Prophets (N'vi-im), and Writings (K'tuvim).

Targumim: Aramaic word for "translations"; refers to either written or spoken translations of the Torah from Hebrew to the vernacular language. One well-known example is Targum Onkelos, a translation into Aramaic.

Tikkun Olam: Hebrew term meaning "repair the world"; often refers to the Jewish call to social justice. Originally a Lurianic Kabbalistic concept, *tikkun olam* referred to scrupulous observance of the commandments in order to repair the brokenness of exilic Jewish life.

Tzaddeket: Hebrew word meaning "righteous woman"; from the same Hebrew root as *tzedek* (justice/righteousness), *tzedakah* (charitable giving), and tzaddik (righteous/holy man).

Vatikot: Hebrew word meaning "elders" (feminine plural); a term of respect for the first female rabbinic ordinees.

Yad: Hebrew word meaning "hand"; usually refers to the pointer— often shaped like an elongated arm tipped by a hand and pointing forefinger—used to read Torah so as not to smudge the ink on the parchment.

Sources and Permissions

3   Rabbi Sally J. Priesand, "A First Step." Excerpted from Rabbi Priesand's Founders Day Speech, delivered March 3, 2022, at HUC–JIR in New York.

4   Rabbi Mary L. Zamore, "Blessed Be the Firsts." Based on a prayer written for the WRJ Jubilee Inaugural, June 6, 2021.

5   Merle Feld, "Let my people go that we may serve You." © Merle Feld, June 2021. Commissioned by Women's Rabbinic Network in honor of Rabbi Sally J. Priesand. Also published in *Longing: Poems of a Life* (New York: CCAR Press, 2023), vii–viii.

24   Alicia Suskin Ostriker, "The Shekhinah as Amnesiac," from *The Volcano Sequence* (Pittsburgh: University of Pittsburgh Press, 2002), 38–40. Reprinted with permission from Alicia Suskin Ostriker.

54   Rabbi Rachel Barenblat, "Mother Psalm 6," from *Waiting to Unfold* (Montreal: Phoenicia Publishing, 2013), 44. Reprinted with permission from Rabbi Rachel Barenblat.

67   Reprinted with permission from the editor's introduction to *Dirshuni: Contemporary Women's Midrash*, ed. Tamar Biala (Waltham, MA: Brandeis University Press, 2022), xxxiv.

80   Erika Dreifus, "Rightful Places." An earlier version of this poem was published in *Lilith*, December 28, 2016, https://lilith.org/2016/12/rightful-places/.

112   Rabbi Karen Bender, "An Offering Made in Honor of Those Who Have No Timem to Make an Offering." This poem was previously published in *CCAR Journal: The Reform Jewish Quarterly: Wisdom You Are My Sister: 25 Years of Women in the Rabbinate*, Summer 1997, 185. It was also published in *The Sacred Calling: Four Decades of Women in the Rabbinate* (New York: CCAR Press, 2016), xlvii–xlviii.

115   Julie R. Enszer, "When the Rabbi Asks for the Envelope." This poem first appeared in *Avowed* (Little Rock, AR: Sibling Rivalry Press, 2016), © Julie R. Enszer, 2023.

119   Nessa Rapoport, "Love As Strong As Death." Reprinted with permission from *A Woman's Book of Grieving* by Nessa Rapoport, linocuts by Rochelle Rubinstein (New York: William Morrow and Company, 1994), 61. © 1994 by Nessa Rapoport. All rights reserved.

About the Editors

Rabbi Sue Levi Elwell, PhD, was the founding director of the Los Angeles Jewish Feminist Center and the first rabbinic director of Ma'yan: The Jewish Women's Project. She is the editor of *Lesbian Rabbis: The First Generation*, *The Open Door: A Passover Haggadah* (CCAR Press, 2002), and *Chapters of the Heart: Jewish Women Sharing the Torah of Our Lives*. Rabbi Elwell has served as a congregational rabbi, worked with congregations, clergy, and lay leaders through the Union for Reform Judaism, and taught in academia and in many communities. Ordained by Hebrew Union College–Jewish Institute of Religion in 1986, she currently serves HUC-JIR as a spiritual director.

Jessica Greenbaum is a poet, teacher, and social worker. She is the author of three books of poems; her most recent, *Spilled and Gone*, was named a Best Book of Poetry by the *Boston Globe* in 2021. Her poems have appeared in the *New Yorker*, *New York Review of Books*, *Poetry*, *Yale Review*, *Paris Review*, and elsewhere. A recipient of awards from the National Endowment for the Arts and the Poetry Society of America, she teaches inside and outside academia, including for Central Synagogue and other Jewish institutions, where her classes pair Jewish text with contemporary poems to renew readers' personal relationships to both. She is the coeditor, with Rabbi Hara E. Person, of *Mishkan HaSeder: A Passover Haggadah* (CCAR Press, 2021).

Rabbi Hara E. Person is the chief executive of the Central Conference of American Rabbis. Previously, she was the CCAR's chief strategy officer, publisher of CCAR Press, and editor-in-chief of URJ Books and Music. Rabbi Person was managing editor of the award-winning *The Torah: A Women's Commentary* (URJ Press and Women of Reform Judaism, 2008) and executive editor of *Mishkan HaNefesh: Machzor for the Days of Awe* (CCAR Press, 2015). Alongside Jessica Greenbaum, she coedited *Mishkan HaSeder: A Passover Haggadah*. Rabbi Person was ordained in 1998 by Hebrew Union College–Jewish Institute of Religion.